The Best Study Series for

GED

Social Studies

Canadian Edition

 With REA's TESTware® on CD-ROM

Colin M. Bain, Ph.D.

 *Research & Education Association*
Visit our website at
www.rea.com

Research & Education Association
61 Ethel Road West
Piscataway, New Jersey 08854
E-mail: info@rea.com

The Best Study Series for the
GED SOCIAL STUDIES TEST–Canadian Edition
With TEST*ware*® **on CD-ROM**

Printed in the United States of America

Library of Congress Control Number 2007933187

ISBN 13: 978-0-7386-0309-4
ISBN 10: 0-7386-0309-0

Windows® is a registered trademark of Microsoft Corporation.

REA® and TEST*ware*® are registered trademarks of
Research & Education Association, Inc.

TABLE OF CONTENTS

Introduction v

    About the Author... vii

    About Research & Education Association... vii

    Acknowledgments.. vii

    About This Book and TEST*ware*®.. viii

    About the GED Program... viii

    About the GED Exam ix

    About the Canadian Social Studies Test ix

    Social Studies Topics x

    When Should I Start Studying?.. xi

    Before the Test xi

    Top Test Tips When Taking the GED xi

    After the Test... xii

    Independent Study Schedule.. xii

Pre-Test 1

    Pre-Test Answer Key...22

    Pre-Test Answers and Explanations 23

Canadian History 31

    Ancient Canada...33

    Canada's Path to a Constitutional Government, 1763–1867 34

    The Age of Macdonald (1867–1891)..36

    Canada in the 20th Century...38

    The First World War (1914–1918) and Canada's Finances 41

    Challenges of the Post–World War II Period, 1945–1976 42

    Failure of the Meech Lake Accord, 1987–1990..44

    Canadian Charter of Rights and Freedoms 45

    Canadian Foreign Policy in the 21st Century 47

Economics 49

    Needs and Wants 51

    Economic Systems..52

    Circular Flow of Economic Activity 54

    Competition...55

    Supply and Demand..57

    Inflation 60

Family Structure and Median Income..62

Economic Themes..63

International Trade Statistics..65

Urbanism and GDP per Capita 66

Civics and Government 69

Nature of Political Systems..71

Canadian Political Process...73

Canadian Political System 75

Elections and Voting Regulations 76

Canadian Political Spectrum..78

"Unite the Right" Campaign, 2000–2004 79

National Executive Branch 80

National Legislative Branch...82

National Judicial Branch...83

Geography 85

Geography Principles and Concepts...87

Canadian Regions 90

Population Growth..93

Population Pyramids 94

Primary, Secondary, and Tertiary Sectors and Gross Domestic Product 95

First Languages...96

Cultural Regions of the World 97

Using the World's Resources 99

Quality-of-Life Indicators..103

United Nations Human Development Index 105

Practice Test 107

Practice Test Answer Key 130

Practice Test Answers and Explanations..131

Post-Test 137

Post-Test Answer Key..165

Post-Test Answers and Explanations 167

Answer Sheets 175

Installing REA's TEST*ware*® 179

Introduction

ABOUT THE AUTHOR

Colin Bain earned his Ph.D. in history from the University of Guelph, Ontario. He taught for 27 years in high schools for the Halton (Ontario) Board of Education. He was a department head (Social Sciences) for 17 years, retiring in 2000. He has been a writer of textbooks and other educational materials since the mid-1970s, with publications to his credit published by Prentice Hall Canada (now Pearson Education Canada), Oxford University Press Canada, as well as Research and Education Association, Inc. Recently, he has developed online distance education courses for the Independent Learning Centre, an organization supported by the Government of Ontario to provide elementary and secondary school credits for people who need them and who have not prospered in traditional learning environments.

ABOUT RESEARCH & EDUCATION ASSOCIATION

Founded in 1959, Research & Education Association (REA) is dedicated to publishing the finest and most effective educational materials—including software, study guides, and test preps—for students in middle school, high school, college, graduate school, and beyond.

REA's Test Preparation series includes books and software for all academic levels in almost all disciplines. Research & Education Association publishes test preps for students who have not yet entered high school, as well as high school students preparing to enter college. For college students seeking advanced degrees, REA publishes test preps for many major graduate school admission examinations in a wide variety of disciplines, including engineering, law, and medicine. Students at every level, in every field, with every ambition can find what they are looking for among REA's publications.

REA's practice tests are always based upon the most recently administered exams, and include every type of question that you can expect on the actual exams.

REA's publications and educational materials are highly regarded and continually receive an unprecedented amount of praise from professionals, instructors, librarians, parents, and students. Our authors are as diverse as the fields represented in the books we publish. They are well-known in their respective disciplines and serve on the faculties of prestigious high schools, colleges, and universities throughout the United States and Canada.

We invite you to visit us at *www.rea.com* to find out how REA is making the world smarter.

ACKNOWLEDGMENTS

Special recognition is extended to the following:

Larry Kling, Vice President, Editorial, for his overall direction.

Pam Weston, Vice President, Publishing, for setting the quality standards for production integrity and managing the publication to completion.

Michael Reynolds, Senior Editor, for project management.

John Paul Cording, Vice President, Technology, for coordinating the design and development of REA's TEST*ware*® software.

Heena Patel, Project Manager, Technology, for software testing and development.

Christine Saul, Senior Graphic Artist, for designing our cover.

Jeff LoBalbo, Senior Graphic Artist, for post-production file mapping.

Matrix Publishing Services, for page design and typesetting the manuscript.

ABOUT THIS BOOK AND TEST*ware*®

This book is designed to help you strengthen the skills you will need to take the GED Canadian Social Studies Test. Thus, it will set you on a path toward earning a GED certificate, which is widely regarded as the equivalent of a high school diploma.

A Pre-Test section in the beginning of this book will help you assess the areas where you need to work the hardest. After you have completed the review areas and answered all of the drill questions, you will be given a Practice Test which will show where you're making good progress and where you still need to study. In the Post-Test section, you will answer questions like those you will face on the actual GED.

Two of the book's three tests are included on the enclosed CD-ROM in our special interactive GED Canadian Social Studies TEST*ware*®. By taking these tests on the computer, you will gain the additional study features and benefits of automatic scoring and enforced time conditions.

The reviews cover all areas tested on the GED Canadian Social Studies Test. Each section contains a drill so you can monitor your progress as you use this book. By mastering the skills presented in this book, you will be able to approach the test with confidence.

ABOUT THE GED PROGRAM

For more than 60 years, the GED Examination has been administered by the GED Testing Service of the American Council on Education (ACE). The GED exam offers anyone who did not complete high school the opportunity to earn a High School Equivalency Certificate. With that certificate come many new opportunities for a better career or higher education.

The GED may be a step on your journey to a college degree, since almost 1 out of every 20 first-year college students has a GED. Or a GED may be your ticket to a better job and into a career with a bright future and room to grow. Whatever your academic or professional goals are, success on the GED is a great place to begin.

The GED exam is available all across Canada. There are over 3,400 testing centers in North America and another 2,800 testing centers worldwide, so you should have no problem finding a GED testing center near you.

For more information on the GED program, to find an administration schedule, or to find a testing center near you, start by contacting your local high school or adult education center. Or, you can contact the American Council on Education, which administers the GED, at:

GED – General Educational Development
American Council on Education
One Dupont Circle NW, Suite 250
Washington, DC 20036-1163

Phone: (202) 939-9300 or
          (800) 626-9433 (Toll Free)

E-mail: comments@ace.nche.edu

Website: *www.gedtest.org*

Alternate-Language GED Tests

If English is not your first language, you may be able to take the GED exam in Spanish or French. Contact the GED administrators for more information.

Accommodations for Test Takers with Disabilities

If you have special needs because of a physical or learning disability, accommodations are available for you. Some examples of qualifying disabilities are blindness, deafness, dyslexia, dyscalculia, and attention-deficit/hyperactivity disorder. A complete list of qualifying disabilities is available from the GED test administrators. The proper accommodations can make a great deal of difference for those entitled to them, so be sure that you are taking the GED exam that's right for you.

If you believe that you have a qualifying disability but you do not have complete documentation, contact the National Rehabilitation Information Center (NARIC) at (800) 346-2742.

ABOUT THE GED EXAM

The GED exam consists of five separate subject tests. The breakdown is outlined in the chart below.

The entire exam is 7 hours and 30 minutes long. That sounds like a lot to cover! But don't worry. Each topic is treated individu-

ally. If you pass all five topics in one sitting, you've earned your GED. If you don't, you only have to retake the section or sections that you did not pass.

A standard score of 450 (out of 800) on each GED test is the minimum passing score set by Canadian jurisdictions.

ABOUT THE CANADIAN SOCIAL STUDIES TEST

The following review has been created to help you become familiar with the types of questions you will encounter on the Social Studies test of the GED Canadian edition. Prior knowledge of the subjects tested is not necessary for you to do well on this exam. The

An Overview of the GED Tests

Test Area	Number of Questions	Time for Test	Test Format
Language Arts, Writing, Part I	50 questions	75 minutes	Organization (15%) Sentence Structure (30%) Usage (30%) Mechanics (25%)
Language Arts, Writing, Part II	1 essay	45 minutes	Written Essay on Assigned Topic
Language Arts, Reading	40 questions	65 minutes	Literary Text (75%) Non-Literary Text (25%)
Mathematics	50 questions	90 minutes	Number Operations and Number Sense (20%–30%) Measurement and Geometry (20%–30%) Data Analysis, Statistics, and Probability (20%–30%) Algebra, Functions, and Patterns (20%–30%)
Social Studies	50 questions	70 minutes	Canadian History (40%) Economics (20%) Civics and Government (25%) Geography (15%)
Science	50 questions	80 minutes	Physical Science (35%) Life Science (45%) Earth and Space Science (20%)

test will require you to read a passage and/or interpret information from a graph, map, or chart, and then answer questions based on that information. This review concentrates on presenting passages and questions similar to those appearing on the GED. By studying the review, you can familiarize yourself with the type of vocabulary that will appear on the test, as well as the content covered.

SOCIAL STUDIES TOPICS

The breakdown below shows the areas covered on the Social Studies test. You should review these topics to accurately answer the questions appearing in this section.

Canadian History (40% of Test)

1. Prehistorical Canada
2. Canada's Native Peoples
3. Canada's Path to a Constitutional Government, 1763–1867
4. Age of Macdonald, 1867–1891
5. Canada in the 20th Century
6. World War I (1914–1918) and Canada's Finances
7. Challenges of the Post–World War II Period, 1945–1976
8. Failure of the Meech Lake Accord, 1987–1990
9. Canadian Charter of Rights and Freedoms
10. Canadian Foreign Policy in the 21st Century

Economics (20% of Test)

1. Needs and Wants
2. Economic Systems
3. Circular Flow of Economic Activity
4. Price and Quantity
5. Supply and Demand
6. Inflation

7. Family Structure and Median Income
8. Employment by Sector
9. International Trade Statistics
10. Urbanism and GDP per Capita

Civics and Government (25% of Test)

1. Nature of Political Systems
2. Canadian Political Process
3. Canadian Political System
4. Elections and Voting Regulations
5. Canadian Political Spectrum
6. "Unite the Right" Campaign, 2000–2004
7. National Executive Branch
8. National Legislative Branch
9. National Judicial Branch

Geography (15% of Test)

1. Geographical Principles and Concepts
2. Canadian Regions
3. Population Growth
4. Population Pyramids
5. Primary, Secondary, and Tertiary Sectors and Gross Domestic Product
6. First Languages
7. Cultural Regions of the World
8. Using the World's Resources
9. Quality-of-Life Indicators
10. United Nations Human Development Index

The more familiar you are with the format of the Social Studies test, the better you will perform. Like the actual test, this review will present you with maps, charts, graphs, and various passages and then ask you questions based on that information given. Although you may feel that you are well prepared for the test, reading this review will help you brush up on your skills and develop speed and accuracy in answering the questions. Also, make sure to memorize the directions to this section so you do not waste valuable time.

WHEN SHOULD I START STUDYING?

If you're wondering when to start studying, the short answer is *now*. You may have a few days, a few weeks, or a few months to prepare for the particular administration of the GED that you're going to take. But in any case, the more time you spend studying for the GED, the better.

BEFORE THE TEST

At some point, you've studied all you can and test day is only one good night's sleep away. Be sure to go to bed early on the night before test day, and get as much rest as you can. Eat a good breakfast. Dress in layers that can be added or removed so you'll be comfortable if the testing center is warmer or cooler than you like. Plan to arrive at the test center at least 20 minutes early so that traffic or other transportation issues don't prevent you from getting to the test center on time. If you're not sure where the test center is, be sure to make the trip at least once before test day. On the morning of test day, your only job is to let nothing—not hunger, not temperature, not traffic—distract you from your main goal: success on the GED. Use the test-day checklist at the back of this book to make sure you've covered all the bases.

What to Bring with You

- Your admission ticket, if you need one
- An official photo ID
- Some sharpened No. 2 pencils (with erasers) and a blue or black ink pen
- A watch, if you have one

The following items will *not* be allowed in the testing area, so if you choose to bring them, know that you will have to store them during the test:

- Purses and tote bags
- Electronic devices, including MP3 players, video games, pagers, cell phones, CD players, etc.
- Food
- Books and notebooks
- Other nonessential items

Remember that by the time you reach test day, you will have put in your study time, taken your practice exams, and learned the test format. You will be calm and confident, knowing that you're ready for the GED.

TOP TEST TIPS WHEN TAKING THE GED

While you're taking the GED, here are some important test strategies:

- Read all the directions carefully so that you understand what's expected of you. If you have questions, ask the GED examiner.

- Answer every question. There's no wrong-answer penalty on the GED, so if you don't know, *guess*. If you leave a question blank, you're guaranteed to get zero points. If you have to guess, you have a 20 per cent chance of getting the question right.

- Smart guesses are better than random guesses. If you have five possible answers, and you have no idea which is correct, that's a random guess. If you have five possible answers and you've eliminated three that are definitely wrong, that's a *smart guess*. You now have a 50 per cent chance of getting the question right.

• Keep an eye on your time. Don't spend too much time on any one question. Choose your best answer, and move on. Come back to troublesome questions later, if there's time.

AFTER THE TEST

When you've completed your GED exam, you've reached the end of one journey and the beginning of another. You gave your best effort and it's a great feeling. Hopefully you've passed all five tests and you can look forward to a new world of opportunity. If you don't pass all five tests, you can focus your study time on only those areas that still need work. But remember, success begins with a goal, and whether you pass on your first try or not, your journey is well under way. Go home, relax, and take a well-deserved rest. You've earned it.

INDEPENDENT STUDY SCHEDULE

The following study schedule allows for thorough preparation for the GED Canadian Social Studies Test. Although it is designed for six weeks, you can customize to fit your schedule. Be sure to set aside enough time (at least two hours each day) to study. But no matter which study schedule works best for you, the more time you spend studying, the more prepared and relaxed you will feel on the day of the exam.

Week	Activity
1	Take our Pre-Test on the enclosed CD-ROM to gauge your basic strengths and weaknesses. You'll now have the basis for determining the areas you need to work on.
2 & 3	Carefully read the review sections of this book, with the chapters titled "Canadian History," "Economics," "Civics and Government," and "Geography."
4	Take the Practice Test in this book. After scoring your exam, carefully review all incorrect answer explanations. If there are any types of questions or particular subjects that seem difficult to you, review those subjects by rereading the appropriate section(s) in this book.
5	Take our Post-Test on the enclosed CD-ROM. Again, after scoring your exam, carefully review all incorrect answer explanations. If there are any types of questions or particular subjects that seem difficult to you, review those subjects by rereading the appropriate section(s) in this book.
6	Devote this week to go over the review material and tests so you are confident about the exam.

GED Social Studies

Pre-Test

PRE-TEST

Directions: Read the information below and then answer the related questions.
Choose the single best answer to each question.

Questions 1 and 2 refer to the following passage.

Macdonald chose to negotiate with the disgruntled Red River Colony in the West; in the Manitoba Act of 1870, the colony became the Province of Manitoba. Many reasons have been given for Macdonald's compromise. Aside from the internal political and religious divisions that were sparked by rebellion, the main issue was the "race" with the United States to occupy and control the West. The Alaska purchase and the discovery of gold in the Yukon brought thousands of Americans north. With the American West beginning to fill, the prairies were seen by many would-be settlers as the "last best West." The remaining independent British colony in North America, British Columbia, was considering joining Canada. It was also under some pressure to join the American union. Thus, Macdonald had every reason to bring the Manitoba issue to a speedy conclusion.

1. What is the main idea of the preceding passage?

   (1) Macdonald made peace with the Red River Colony to expedite Canadian expansion into the West; his greatest fear was that the United States would advance into the Northwest first.

   (2) Macdonald wanted to avoid further confrontation with the Red River Colony, primarily because of an abundance of problems he was already experiencing in the East.

   (3) Macdonald was concerned with beating the United States to the Alaska purchase, thereby preserving Yukon gold for Canada.

   (4) British Columbia was an independent British colony that wished to remain independent, despite Macdonald's entreaties.

   (5) The Manitoba issue was not of a particular concern to Macdonald; he therefore dismissed the issue without initiating a major confrontation with the Red River Colony.

2. The preceding passage might imply that Macdonald

   (1) was unconcerned with matters of the West.

   (2) had always been fond of the Red River Colony.

   (3) was eager to expand Canada before it was too late.

   (4) had no desire whatsoever to bring British Columbia into Canada.

   (5) had no reason to feel competitive with Canada's neighbor, the United States.

Question 3 refers to the following passage.

The first plank of Macdonald's "National Policy" was complete. The second was protective tariffs to encourage a domestic manufacturing industry. The third was the settlement of the West—the issue that caused the old problems of language and religion to return with a vengeance.

When the Hudson's Bay Company had transferred its vast territory of the Northwest to Canada, no steps were taken to inform the people of Red River. More than half of them were French-speaking Métis, who were Roman Catholics. They feared being submerged by an influx of English-speaking Protestants. Anxious to protect their lands, language, and religion, they turned to Louis Riel for leadership. On November 2, 1869, Riel seized Fort Garry and established a provisional government, with himself as head. When the Canadian government responded by sending an army west to put down the rebellion, Riel fled to the United States.

In 1885 the Métis' grievances caused Riel to return. He proclaimed a provisional government in March 1885, but it was short lived. Riel was executed at Regina in November, causing a split in the country between English-speaking Protestants who clamoured for his death and French speaking Catholics who had asked for clemency.

3. The execution of Louis Riel

(1) made him an example of inequality to the French and Catholics.

(2) demonstrated Macdonald's determination to settle the West.

(3) marked the beginning of the end of the Méti and Indian cultures in the Western settlements.

(4) virtually eliminated the Conservative Party as a force in Quebec until the end of the Second World War.

(5) All of the above

Question 4 refers to the following passage.

At the end of the Second World War, Europe was largely destroyed, and the Soviet Union and communism were regarded as the new "enemy." On April 4, 1949, Canada and 15 other western countries signed the North Atlantic Treaty, forming the North Atlantic Treaty Organization (NATO). With this alliance the member countries promised to consider an attack on any one of them as an attack on them all. In 1957 the Soviet Union's launching of the satellite *Sputnik* and its development of atom and hydrogen bombs led to the formation of the North American Aerospace Defense Command (NORAD) through an agreement between Canada and the United States signed in 1958.

Canada's role in world affairs was also seen in the Commonwealth. In the postwar period Canada played a leading role in keeping former colonies—now new countries—within the Commonwealth. By so doing, it transformed the Commonwealth into a multiracial association.

4. All the following factored into Canada's decision to join NORAD **except**

(1) the launch of *Sputnik*.

(2) the development of nuclear weapons by the Soviet Union.

(3) Canada's participation in NATO.

(4) Canada's leading role in keeping developing countries in the British Commonwealth.

(5) Stalin's domination of Eastern Europe after the Second World War.

Questions 5–7 refer to the following table.

**Number of People Moving into and out of
Selected Canadian Provinces, 1977–2000**

Years	Manitoba	Ontario	Alberta	British Columbia	Saskatchewan
1977–1981	–42 115	–60 890	190 719	131 176	–11 729
1982–1986	–2395	65 460	–82 737	3226	–7057
1987–1991	–39 533	28 876	–13 198	154 126	–69 397
1992–1995	–18 997	–32 592	242	135 036	–19 418
1996–2000	–16 292	48 889	127 053	–17 017	–19 521
Totals	–114 542	49 743	222 079	406 547	–127 122

5. Which province experienced the largest net increase in population from 1977 to 2000?

(1) Manitoba

(2) Ontario

(3) Alberta

(4) British Columbia

(5) Saskatchewan

6. Which province experienced the most periods of population increase?

(1) Manitoba

(2) Ontario

(3) Alberta

(4) British Columbia

(5) Saskatchewan

7. Which province experienced the greatest net population increase in a single period?

(1) Manitoba

(2) Ontario

(3) Alberta

(4) British Columbia

(5) Saskatchewan

Question 8 refers to the following table.

**Canada's Consumer Price Index (CPI),
1992 and 2003**

Year	CPI
1992	100
2003	123

8. By how much did Canada's prices increase between 1992 and 2003?

(1) 230 per cent

(2) 123 per cent

(3) 23 per cent

(4) 2.3 per cent

(5) 0.23 per cent

Questions 9 and 10 refer to the following table.

Federal Election Results, 1926–1945

Year	Liberal	Conservative	Co-operative Commonwealth Federation (CCF)	Social Credit	Others	Total
1925	101	116	0	0	28	245
1926	116	91	0		38	245
1930	88	137	0		20	245
1935	171	39	7	17	1	245
1940	178	39	8	10	10	245

9. In which year did the Conservatives win a majority government?

   (1) 1925

   (2) 1926

   (3) 1930

   (4) 1935

   (5) 1940

10. The table shows the performance of the CCF in the elections of 1935 and 1940. Founded in 1933, the CCF changed its name in 1961 when it formed a partnership with the labour union movement. It survives today under a new name and won seats in Parliament in every general election from 1963 to 2000. What is its new name?

   (1) Canadian Alliance

   (2) Progressive Conservatives

   (3) New Democratic Party

   (4) Family Coalition Party

   (5) Green Party

Questions 11 and 12 refer to the following table.

Canadian Government Revenues and Expenditures in Selected Years, 1891–1971

Year	Revenues (in millions of Canadian dollars)	Expenditures (in millions of Canadian dollars)
1891	58	39
1911	118	145
1931	872	749
1951	3113	1296
1971	12 803	14 416

11. According to the table, in which year did the federal government record its first deficit?

    (1) 1891

    (2) 1911

    (3) 1931

    (4) 1951

    (5) 1971

12. In which year did the federal government have its largest surplus?

    (1) 1891

    (2) 1911

    (3) 1931

    (4) 1951

    (5) 1971

Questions 13–15 refer to the following passage and cartoon.

> In 1980 the government of Quebec held a referendum of its population to gain support for its attempts at negotiating a "sovereignty association" agreement with the rest of Canada and establishing Quebec as a separate country.

The cartoon that follows appeared in the *Vancouver Sun* at that time.

The Canadianese Twins

Source: Roy Peterson OC, The Vancouver Sun.

13. Who are the two people in the cartoon?

    (1) Ronald Reagan and Pierre Trudeau

    (2) Pierre Trudeau and Brian Mulroney

    (3) Brian Mulroney and René Lévesque

    (4) René Lévesque and Pierre Trudeau

    (5) René Lévesque and Ronald Reagan

14. What is the cartoonist saying about the issue?

    (1) Quebec would get the best deal from sovereignty association.

    (2) Quebec is going to win this contest.

    (3) Canada would get the best deal from sovereignty association.

    (4) Quebec and Canada both have much to gain from sovereignty association.

    (5) Canada is going to win this contest.

15. After the Quebec referendum rejected sovereignty association in 1981, what major change did the government of Canada introduce in 1982 in an attempt to weaken Quebec separatism?

    (1) Free Trade Agreement (FTA) with the United States

    (2) Patriation of the constitution and the introduction of the Charter of Rights and Freedoms

    (3) North American Free Trade Agreement (NAFTA) with the United States and Mexico

    (4) Medicare system across Canada

    (5) Kyoto Agreement

Questions 16–18 refer to the following table.

Principal Religious Denominations of the Population, Canada, 1871, 1901, and 1951

Denomination	1871	1901	1951
Anglican	501 269	681 494	2 060 720
Baptist	243 714	318 005	519 585
Lutheran	37 935	92 524	444 923
Presbyterian	574 577	842 531	781 747
Roman Catholic	1 532 471	2 229 600	6 069 496

16. Which was the largest denomination in 1901?

    (1) Anglican

    (2) Baptist

    (3) Lutheran

    (4) Presbyterian

    (5) Roman Catholic

17. In percentage terms, which denomination grew the most between 1871 and 1901?

    (1) Anglican

    (2) Baptist

    (3) Lutheran

    (4) Presbyterian

    (5) Roman Catholic

18. Which denomination grew the least in total numbers between 1871 and 1951?

    (1) Anglican

    (2) Baptist

    (3) Lutheran

    (4) Presbyterian

    (5) Roman Catholic

Questions 19 and 20 refer to the following map and passage.

Map of Quebec Following the Quebec Act of 1774

General James Murray, the first civil governor of Quebec, found himself torn between a growing British minority, which wanted more power, and the French majority, which wanted guarantees that their laws, institutions, and religion would prevail. Murray's successor, Colonel Guy Carleton, was determined that the French would be well treated, especially with the American colonies showing signs of rebellion and the defence of Quebec becoming crucial. His efforts resulted in the passing of the Quebec Act in 1774. The act gave Roman Catholics the right to hold public office and legalized the levying of tithes by the Catholic Church. French civil law was continued and the French language officially recognized. Government leadership would remain with the governor and a council, but there would be no elected assembly.

19. The Quebec Act of 1774

    (1) gave Roman Catholics in Quebec permission to hold public office and levy tithes.

    (2) retained French civil law and recognized the French language in Quebec.

    (3) allowed Roman Catholics to serve in the elected assembly.

    (4) provided for all the above.

    (5) provided for both (1) and (2).

20. What would be the most important change made to the boundaries shown in the map after the American Revolutionary War and acknowledged in the Constitutional Act of 1791?

    (1) Newfoundland was given to France.

    (2) The land south of the Great Lakes was given to the United States.

    (3) The land belonging to the Hudson's Bay Company was purchased by Canada.

    (4) Nova Scotia was given to Spain.

    (5) Ottawa became the capital of Canada.

Questions 21 and 22 refer to the following passage.

The governments within Canada's borders are elected into power because of their commitments to preserve the general well-being of their constituencies. Federal revenues and expenditures must work toward that end.

Economic stability is a principal goal for the government because the economy greatly affects the happiness of the people. Voters do not tolerate a government that does not achieve a good standard of living for its citizens. Fiscal policy is the government's management of tax revenues and expenditures; it is a powerful tool that influences economic stability. The federal government's expenditures involve unconditional equalization payments from the richer provinces to the poorer ones to maintain a standard and uniform level of federal services. Federal expenditures provide conditional grants for hospitalization insurance, medicare, and postsecondary education. Federal expenditures also support unemployed persons while they seek new jobs that would enable them to attain economic and social stability. The federal government's employment insurance (EI) programs support both unemployed persons and people retraining for the workplace. Those who become discouraged and are ineligible for EI payments can receive welfare payments from the provincial government.

21. Which of the following is **not** an example of a federal expenditure used to ensure economic stability?

    (1) Funding poorer provinces with taxes from richer ones

    (2) Providing grants for college tuition

    (3) Supporting unemployed citizens

    (4) Purchasing defence equipment

    (5) Funding grants for medicare

22. EI support is available for unemployed people who are

    (1) enrolled in job-training programs.

    (2) in need of financial aid for college.

    (3) receiving welfare payments from the provincial government.

    (4) seeking hospitalization insurance.

    (5) none of the above.

Questions 23 and 24 refer to the following table.

Average Earnings of the Canadian Population 15 Years and Older by Highest Level of Schooling, 2001

All levels	31 757
High school graduation certificate and/or some postsecondary school	25 477
Trades certificate or diploma	32 743
College certificate or diploma	32 736
University certificate, diploma, or degree	48 648

23. Which conclusion may be correctly drawn from the table?

    (1) There is no relationship between levels of education and average income.

    (2) College certificate or diploma holders earn less than the average for all levels of education.

    (3) The higher the education level you have, the more likely you are to achieve a high income.

    (4) People who graduate from high school and/or pursue some postsecondary education earn more on average than people with trades certificates or diplomas.

    (5) People with university certificates, diplomas, or degrees earn more than twice as much on average as people with trades certificates or diplomas.

24. For which educational groups is the average income less than that for all levels of education?

    (1) High school graduation certificate and/or some postsecondary education

    (2) Trades certificate or diploma

    (3) College certificate or diploma

    (4) University certificate, diploma, or degree

    (5) None of the above

Questions 25–27 refer to the following passage and table.

The national statistics-reporting agency Statistics Canada regularly monitors major economic indicators about Canadian families. One item it measures is median family income. The following table indicates some of the findings about Canadian family income, as it relates to family size, between 1980 and 2000.

Median Incomes of Canadian Census Families, 1980, 1990, and 2000

Census family type*	Median income†			Percentage change
	1980	1990	2000	
All	51 698	54 560	55 016	0.8
Couple families with no children	46 190	49 071	50 509	2.9
Couple families with at least one child under 18 years	57 515	62 326	65 962	5.8
Couple families whose children are all 18 years and older	73 524	77 810	80 545	3.5
Lone-parent families with at least one child under 18 years	20 815	21 797	26 008	19.3
Lone-parent families whose children are all 18 years and older	41 423	42 907	43 187	0.7

*Families living in single-family households with no additional persons, such as grandparents, uncles, and aunts.
†Median incomes are expressed in constant 2000 Canadian dollars before income tax is deducted.

25. What do you think Statistics Canada means by the term *median income* of each family type?

    (1) The total income of that family type divided by the number of families

    (2) The average income of that family type

    (3) The income at which 50 per cent of families of that type earn more and 50 per cent of families earn less

    (4) The level of income necessary to sustain a family of that type adequately

    (5) The level of income remaining after families pay their taxes

26. Which family type experienced the smallest percentage income gain between 1990 and 2000?

    (1) Couple families with no children

    (2) Couple families with at least one child under 18 years

    (3) Couple families whose children are all 18 years and older

    (4) Lone-parent families with at least one child under 18 years

    (5) Lone-parent families whose children are all 18 years and older

27. Which family type earned closest to the median income in 1990?

    (1) Couple families with no children

    (2) Couple families with at least one child under 18 years

    (3) Couple families whose children are all 18 years and older

    (4) Lone-parent families with at least one child under 18 years

    (5) Lone-parent families whose children are all 18 years and older

Questions 28–30 refer to the following graphs.

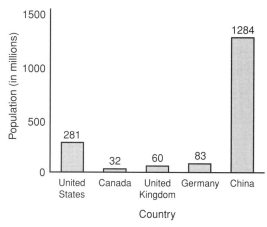

Populations of Five Major Countries, 2003

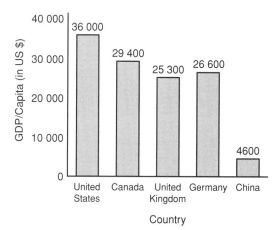

Gross Domestic Product (GDP) per capita of Five Major Countries, 2003

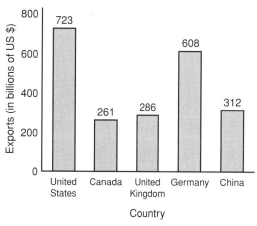

Annual Exports of Five Major Countries, 2003

28. Which statement can correctly be inferred from the graphs?

    (1) Canada has the highest GDP per capita.

    (2) Canada has the largest population.

    (3) China is the largest exporter.

    (4) The United Kingdom has the smallest population.

    (5) Germany has the second-highest exports.

29. Which statement can correctly be inferred from the graphs?

    (1) Canada's population is less than half that of Germany.

    (2) China's population is more than six times as large as that of the United States.

    (3) Germany's GDP per capita is more than seven times as large as that of China.

    (4) The United Kingdom's exports are less than half those of Germany.

    (5) Canada's exports are more than half those of the United States.

30. Of the items listed in the bar graphs, which would be the best indicator of the people's standard of living?

    (1) GDP per capita

    (2) Annual exports divided by population

    (3) Annual exports

    (4) Annual exports divided by GDP per capita

    (5) GDP per capita multiplied by population

Questions 31–33 refer to the following passage.

The legislative branch consists of the Senate and the House of Commons, known collectively as the Canadian Parliament. The House of Commons is the popularly elected lower house, often considered to be an uncontrolled arena of liberalism. The Senate is the upper house and is regarded as a place of "sober second thought." This bicameral ("two-house") legislature exists in approximately 50 countries around the world.

The Senate considers legislation that has been prepared by parliamentary committees and the public service and has been approved by the Cabinet and the House of Commons. The Senate can approve, reject, or amend the bills it receives. If a bill is approved by both houses, it is sent to the governor-general, who will then sign it in the presence of both houses. Once the governor-general signs the bill, it has "royal assent" and becomes law. The bill then changes to an act; for example, Bill 99 would become Act 99.

31. What does the passage imply when it mentions that a bicameral legislature exists in roughly 50 countries worldwide?

    (1) Bicameral legislatures are too widespread to be effective.

    (2) A bicameral legislature is the oldest form of government.

    (3) A bicameral legislature loses its effectiveness over time.

    (4) Canada should develop a more unique form of government.

    (5) The worldwide use of the bicameral legislature is a sign of its effectiveness.

32. Which of the following is a usual step that occurs before the Senate determines the value of a bill it receives?

    (1) Her Majesty the Queen rereads the bill.

    (2) The prime minister, as well as the other cabinet ministers, approves the bill.

    (3) The House of Commons approves the bill.

    (4) Both (2) and (3)

    (5) All of the above

33. What does the term "uncontrolled arena of liberalism" imply about the House of Commons?

    (1) The House of Commons is inhabited only by the Liberal Party.

    (2) The House of Commons is lawless and disorganized.

    (3) The House of Commons is less conservative than the Senate.

    (4) Liberalism is needed to control the House of Commons.

    (5) Liberalism is as prevalent in the Senate as in the House of Commons, but it is more controlled in the Senate.

Question 34 refers to the following passage and cartoon.

> In 2003 the United States, with support of a coalition composed of Britain, Australia, and other countries, invaded Iraq. After the coalition ousted the government of Saddam Hussein, the Iraqis held an election and established an administration structured along democratic ideals. However, groups within Iraq oppose the newly established government, and internal disorder continues. As a result of its actions in Iraq, the U.S. government experienced serious disagreements with allies such as France and Germany. The following cartoon refers to this situation.

Reprinted with permission from the Globe and Mail.

34. Who is the person on the left side of the picture?

    (1) Prime Minister Paul Martin

    (2) Chancellor Gerhard Schroeder

    (3) President Jacques Chirac

    (4) Prime Minister Tony Blair

    (5) President George W. Bush

Questions 35 and 36 refer to the following voter registration information.

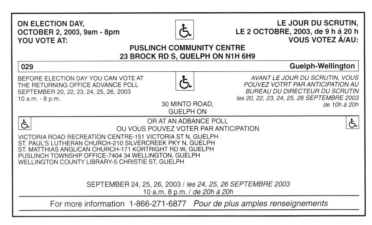

ON ELECTION DAY, OCTOBER 2, 2003, 9am - 8pm YOU VOTE AT:	♿	LE JOUR DU SCRUTIN, LE 2 OCTOBRE, 2003, de 9 h á 20 h VOUS VOTEZ Á/AU:

PUSLINCH COMMUNITY CENTRE
23 BROCK RD S, QUELPH ON N1H 6H9

029		Guelph-Wellington
BEFORE ELECTION DAY YOU CAN VOTE AT THE RETURNING OFFICE ADVANCE POLL SEPTEMBER 20, 22, 23, 24, 25, 26, 2003 10 a.m. - 8 p.m.	♿ 30 MINTO ROAD, GUELPH ON	AVANT LE JOUR DU SCRUTIN, VOUS POUVEZ VOTRT PAR ANTICIPATION AU BUREAU DU DIRECTEUR DU SCRUTIN les 20, 22, 23, 24, 25, 26 SEPTEMBRE 2003 de 10h á 20h

♿ OR AT AN ADBANCE POLL ♿
OU VOUS POUVEZ VOTER PAR ANTICIPATION
VICTORIA ROAD RECREATION CENTRE-151 VICTORIA ST N, GUELPH
ST. PAUL'S LUTHERAN CHURCH-210 SILVERCREEK PKY N, GUELPH
ST. MATTHIAS ANGLICAN CHURCH-171 KORTRIGHT RD W, GUELPH
PUSLINCH TOWNSHIP OFFICE-7404 34 WELLINGTON, GUELPH
WELLINGTON COUNTY LIBRARY-5 CHRISTIE ST, GUELPH

SEPTEMBER 24, 25, 26, 2003 / les 24, 25, 26 SEPTEMBRE 2003
10 a.m. 8 p.m. / de 20h á 20h

For more information 1-866-271-6877 *Pour de plus amples renseignements*

Voter Registration Information, 2006

35. For how many days are the advance polls open?

    (1) 2 days

    (2) 4 days

    (3) 6 days

    (4) 8 days

    (5) 10 days

36. The voter registration card is for the Ontario provincial election of October 2003. Which of the following statements is **incorrect**, based on the information contained in the card?

    (1) Advance polling hours are 10 a.m. to 8 p.m.

    (2) People with disabilities will not be able to vote.

    (3) Advance polls will be held at five locations.

    (4) Polling hours on election day are 9 a.m. to 8 p.m.

    (5) The information on the card is provided in English only.

Question 37 refers to the following diagram.

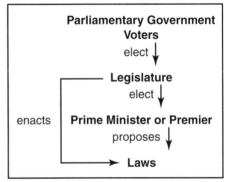

Interactions among the Crown, House of Commons, and Senate

37. In the diagram what is the first body that must approve a bill as it moves through the stages to become a law?

    (1) Governor-general

    (2) Senate

    (3) House of Commons

    (4) Cabinet

    (5) Parliament

Questions 38 and 39 refer to the following table.

Result of the Federal General Election, Canada, 2006

Party	Number of seats	Percentage of popular vote
Bloc Québécois	51	10.5%
Conservatives	124	36.3%
Greens	0	4.5%
Independents	1	1.0%
Liberals	103	30.2%
New Democratic Party	29	17.5%
Totals	308	100.0%

38. Which party formed the government after the election, based on the results?

   (1) Bloc Québécois

   (2) Conservatives

   (3) Independents

   (4) Liberals

   (5) New Democratic Party

39. Which party won the most seats in relation to the percentage of the popular vote it gathered?

   (1) Bloc Québécois

   (2) Conservatives

   (3) Independents

   (4) Liberals

   (5) New Democratic Party

Questions 40 and 41 refer to the following passage.

In 1798 Thomas Malthus, an Englishman who earned a degree in mathematics at Cambridge but became an Anglican parson, predicted how population and food supply would grow. He theorized that population growth would follow a geometric sequence (1, 2, 4, 8, 16, 32, etc.), while food supply would expand in an arithmetical sequence (1, 2, 3, 4, 5, 6, etc.).

40. What conclusion could logically be drawn from Malthus's theory?

   (1) Each member of the population will have more food in the future.

   (2) Each member of the population will have the same amount of food in the future.

   (3) Food and population will grow at the same rate in the future.

   (4) Each member of the population will have less food in the future.

   (5) Food production will grow faster than population in the future.

41. Which of the following events would help to reduce the problem that Malthus identified in analyzing the growth of population and food supply?

   (1) Families having more babies

   (2) Men and women marrying younger

   (3) Bad harvests as a result of inadequate rainfall

   (4) Families being limited to one child

   (5) People living longer

Questions 42–44 refer to the following climate graphs.

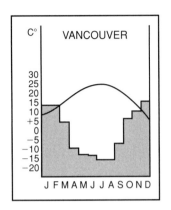 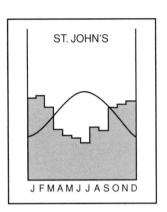 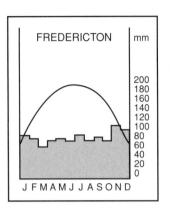

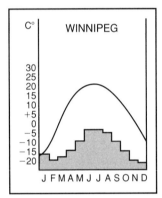 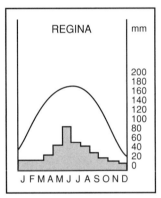

**Climate Graphs of Five Canadian Cities,
Showing Temperature (left scale) and Precipitation (right scale)**
*Shaded areas represent rainfall.

42. Which city experiences the highest rainfall in July?

    (1) Vancouver

    (2) St. John's

    (3) Fredericton

    (4) Winnipeg

    (5) Regina

43. Which city is coldest in January?

    (1) Vancouver

    (2) St. John's

    (3) Fredericton

    (4) Winnipeg

    (5) Regina

44. Which city is most likely to have its climate moderated by ocean currents?

    (1) Vancouver

    (2) St. John's

    (3) Fredericton

    (4) Winnipeg

    (5) Regina

Questions 45 and 46 refer to the following graph and passage.

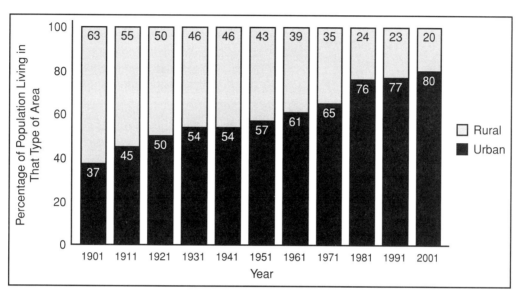

Canadian Population Trends, 1901–2001

The Canadian census is taken every year ending in 1. Among other things, the censuses show that the mix of urban and rural population has changed substantially and consistently since 1901.

45. Which would be the most detailed alternative title for the bar graph?

   (1) Trends in Rural Settlements

   (2) Trends in Urban Settlements

   (3) 20th-Century Population Trends

   (4) Population Growth Trends

   (5) Urban and Rural Populations as Percentages of Total, 1901–2001

46. Which development in the Canadian population between 1901 and 2001 **cannot** be inferred from the graph?

   (1) Growth of large cities

   (2) Decline of farms

   (3) Development of a multicultural nation

   (4) Abandonment of some isolated communities

   (5) Expansion of some towns into cities

Question 47 refers to the following table.

World Population Growth since 1 c.e.

Year	Population (in millions)
1	300
1000	400
1500	440
1800	800
1900	1600
1950	2500
2000	6000

47. Which of the following conclusions may be correctly drawn from the table?

   (1) The fastest increase in population took place between 1800 and 1900.

   (2) Since 1800, population has grown at an increasing rate.

   (3) The population in 2000 was more than 25 times the population in 1 c.e.

   (4) The trend since 1950 provides optimism that world population growth is slowing.

   (5) The slowest increase in population took place between 1500 and 1800.

Question 48 refers to the following passage and table.

A nation's fertility rate is the number of live births the average female member of the population will produce in her lifetime. The table shows how these can vary among nations and periods.

Fertility Rates in Five Countries, 1960, 1980, 2000, and 2050 (Predicted)

Country	1960	1980	2000	2050
A	3.8	1.7	1.64	1.70
B	2.8	1.9	1.75	1.70
C	6.2	6.5	6.08	2.75
D	3.5	1.8	2.06	2.22
E	6.2	4.0	2.13	1.70

48. Which nation is **most** likely to be an agricultural nation with a low standard of living?

   (1) A

   (2) B

   (3) C

   (4) D

   (5) E

Questions 49 and 50 refer to the following passage and table.

Demographers are people who study population information and statistics. Many have also studied geography. Projecting current population trends into the future allows demographers to predict what the populations of countries will look like in two or three generations. The graph illustrates what demographers were predicting at the beginning of the 20th century.

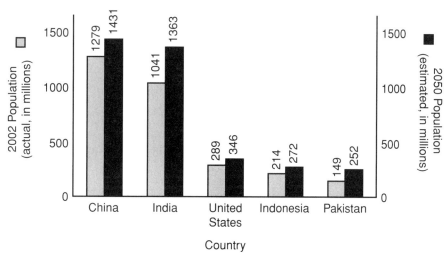

Most Populated Countries, 2002 and 2050

49. Which country will likely experience the largest growth in population between 2002 and 2050?

    (1) China

    (2) India

    (3) United States

    (4) Indonesia

    (5) Pakistan

50. Of these countries, which would be considered a developed, industrial nation?

    (1) China

    (2) India

    (3) United States

    (4) Indonesia

    (5) Pakistan

PRE-TEST

ANSWER KEY

1. (1)	14. (1)	27. (1)	40. (4)
2. (3)	15. (2)	28. (5)	41. (4)
3. (5)	16. (5)	29. (1)	42. (3)
4. (4)	17. (3)	30. (1)	43. (4)
5. (4)	18. (4)	31. (5)	44. (1)
6. (4)	19. (5)	32. (4)	45. (5)
7. (3)	20. (2)	33. (3)	46. (3)
8. (3)	21. (4)	34. (5)	47. (2)
9. (3)	22. (1)	35. (3)	48. (3)
10. (3)	23. (3)	36. (2)	49. (2)
11. (2)	24. (1)	37. (4)	50. (3)
12. (4)	25. (3)	38. (2)	
13. (4)	26. (5)	39. (1)	

PRE-TEST ANSWERS AND EXPLANATIONS

1. **(1)** This answer best sums up the two main points expanded on throughout the passage. (2) The passage never implies that Macdonald had problems in the East. (3) Nor does it suggest that Macdonald was after Yukon gold. (4) British Columbia was clearly on the brink of choosing one country or another; therefore, it had no desire to remain independent. (5) The Manitoba issue was certainly a concern to Macdonald, as the conflict was a detriment to Canadian expansion in the West.

2. **(3)** Clearly, Canada's western expansion was a chief concern to Macdonald, especially because it was also a major interest of the United States (1). Nowhere does the passage suggest particular affinity held by Macdonald for the Red River Colony (2). He most certainly wanted to annex British Columbia into Canada (4), and this and other western interests gave him every reason to feel competitive against the United States (5).

3. **(5)** All the results listed occurred. When Riel was found guilty of treason (1), members of the jury—who believed Riel was insane and who were probably fearful of a French and Catholic backlash—unanimously recommended a light sentence. The judge in the case, however, ordered Riel to hang, under pressure from Macdonald's government. The execution was (and still is) seen as an example to the French and Catholics of the inequality they suffered under the new government, dominated by the English and Protestants. (2) Macdonald wanted to show that he was determined to settle the West and to hold Riel up as an example for anyone who would try to stop him. (3) The death of Riel opened the door to vast expansion and development of the West, and resulted in the eventual destruction of the Métis and Indian cultures in these lands. (4) In response to Macdonald's demanding Riel's death sentence, his subsequent refusal to commute it, and the backing he received from the Conservative Party, the French in Quebec voted the Conservatives out and kept them out until 1945.

4. **(4)** Canada did take a leading role in keeping developing countries in the British Commonwealth, but this was an economic matter for Canada, Britain, and the new nations and did not involve Cold War issues. (3) The Soviet Union refused to leave the territory it occupied in Eastern Europe at the end of the Second World War, saying it needed border protection, but in fact treated these nations as conquered states. This raised fears that Stalin would march across Europe and turn on North America. (1 and 2) The Soviet Union's further development of nuclear weapons and the launch of the *Sputnik* satellite—which, it was feared, could carry nuclear weapons—prompted the formation of NATO as a common defence pact between Western Europe, the United States, and Canada. All these threats from the Soviets prompted Canada and the United States to form NORAD, the North American Aerospace Defense Command, to protect themselves from possible Soviet attack.

5. **(4)** British Columbia experienced a net increase of 406 547. (1) Manitoba had a net decrease of 114 542. (2) Ontario had a net increase of 49 743. (3) Alberta had a net in-

crease of 222 079. (5) Saskatchewan had a net decrease of 127 122.

6. **(4)** British Columbia experienced only one period of population decrease (1996–2000). All other provinces experienced more periods of population decrease than this. (1) Manitoba had five such periods (1977–1981, 1982–1986, 1987–1991, 1992–1995, and 1996–2000). (2) Ontario had two (1977–1981 and 1992–1995). (3) Alberta had two (1982–1986 and 1987–1991). (5) Saskatchewan had five (1977–1981, 1982–1986, 1987–1991, 1992–1995, and 1996–2000).

7. **(3)** Alberta experienced a net increase of 190 719 between 1977 and 1981. (1) Manitoba's population has decreased in the years covered in this table. (2) Ontario's largest net increase was 65 460 (1982–1986). (4) British Columbia's largest net increase was 154 126 (1987–1991). (5) Saskatchewan did not experience any period of net population increase.

8. **(3)** The change in real cost is found by identifying the difference between the base year (1992) and the current year (2003). Therefore, 123 − 100 = 23, or 23 per cent of the first number, 100.

9. **(3)** To win a majority government, a party must win more than half the total 245 seats in the House of Commons, or at least 123 seats. The Conservatives won 137 seats in 1930, giving them a majority government. (2, 4, and 5) In the years indicated the Liberals won more seats than any other party and became the government. (1) Although the Conservatives won more seats than any other party and became the government in 1925, they won fewer than 123 seats and were therefore a minority government.

10. **(3)** The CCF became the New Democratic Party in 1961. (1) The Canadian Alliance was formed out of the Reform Party in 1999. (2) The Conservatives became the Progressive Conservatives when they merged with the Progressives in 1945. They became the Conservatives again in 2003 when they merged with the Canadian Alliance. (4 and 5) The Family Coalition Party and the Green Party were not formed out of other parties and have never won seats in Parliament.

11. **(2)** A deficit is when a government spends more than it collects in revenues. In 1911 the government spent $145 million, which was more than the $118 million it collected, thus recording a deficit for the first time. (1) In 1891 it had a surplus because it collected more than it spent. (3) It also had a surplus in 1931. (4 and 5) It had deficits in 1951 and 1971, but those occurred after its deficit in 1911.

12. **(4)** By subtracting expenditures from revenues, we can calculate the surpluses or deficits. (Here, as in the table, all figures are in millions of Canadian dollars.) In 1951 Canada had a surplus of $3113 − $1296 = $1817. (1) In 1891 the surplus was $58 − $39 = $19. (2) 1911 shows a deficit, because $118 − $145 = −$27. (3) In 1931 Canada had a surplus of $872 − $749 = $123. (5) The year 1971 shows a deficit of $12 803 − $14 416 = −$1613.

13. **(4)** Pierre Trudeau (shown on the left in the cartoon) was prime minister of Canada in 1980, and René Lévesque (right) was premier of Quebec. They were the major players in this political contest. The other answers are incorrect because Ronald Reagan was the U.S. president at the time, and Brian Mulroney did not become prime minister until 1984; therefore, neither was involved in the issue.

14. **(1)** The writing in the cartoon is supposed to have come from Lévesque. He means that he wants Quebec to be a separate country but still to receive money from Canada's government. If that were to happen, Quebec would get the best deal, so (3) and (4) are clearly incorrect. The cartoon does not predict who will win the contest, so (2) and (5) are also incorrect.

15. **(2)** The patriation (bringing home from Britain) of the constitution and the introduction of the Charter of Rights and Freedoms were designed to give greater independence to Canada while giving greater protection to individual rights than had previously been the case. Prime Minister Trudeau hoped that this would give Quebeckers a stronger identification with Canada. (1) The FTA was signed in 1989 and dealt with Canada's international trade. (3) NAFTA was signed in 1993 and also dealt with international trade. (4) The medicare system came into effect in the 1960s and had nothing to do with Quebec separatism. (5) Canada signed the Kyoto Agreement in 2000, but it deals with reducing greenhouse gases.

16. **(5)** is correct. There were 2 229 600 Roman Catholics in 1901. (1) There were 681 494 Anglicans, (2) 318 005 Baptists, (3) 92 524 Lutherans, and (4) 842 531 Presbyterians.

17. **(3)** Lutherans grew by 144 per cent. Using the formula (1901 number − 1871 number)/1871 number × 100, (92 524 − 37 935)/37 935 × 100 = 143.9 percent. The other figures are: (1) Anglican 35.9 per cent, (2) Baptist 30.5 percent, (4) Presbyterian 46.6 per cent, (5) Roman Catholic 45.5 per cent.

18. **(4)** is correct. By subtracting the 1871 figures from the 1951 figures (781 747 −

574 577) we see that Presbyterians grew by 207 170 people. (1) Anglicans grew by 1 559 451; (2) Baptists grew by 275 821; (3) Lutherans by 406 988; (5) Roman Catholics grew by 4 537 025.

19. **(5)** The Quebec Act was passed by Governor Guy Carleton in 1774 as a way of appeasing the French in Quebec, thereby ensuring its defence from the rebellious Americans. The act gave Roman Catholics in Quebec permission to hold public office and levy tithes and retained French civil law and recognized the French language in Quebec. However, the governor dictated the law in the Canadian colonies, so there was no elected assembly.

20. **(2)** The land south of the Great Lakes was acknowledged to belong to the United States. The states of Ohio and Michigan were eventually established there. (1) is incorrect because Newfoundland remained a British colony until it became part of Canada in 1949. (3) Eventually, Canada did purchase land belonging to the Hudson's Bay Company but not until the 1870s, when Canada had become independent. (4) Nova Scotia remained a British colony until it became part of Canada in 1867. (5) Ottawa was not the capital until 1867, when Canada became an independent nation.

21. **(4)** Purchasing defence equipment is not mentioned at all in the passage. Funding poorer provinces (1), providing grants for post-secondary education (2), assisting unemployed citizens (3), and providing grants for medicare (5) are all mentioned in the passage as being federal expenditures used to ensure economic stability.

22. **(1)** The passage specifically mentions that EI supports those who are "retraining for

the workplace." College financial aid (2) and hospitalization insurance (4) have nothing to do with EI. Those receiving welfare payments from the provincial government failed to qualify for EI support (3). Because (1) is correct, (5) must be incorrect.

23. **(3)** The higher the education level you have, the more likely you are to achieve a high income. Since this answer is true, answer (1) must logically be false. College certificate or diploma holders ($32 736) earn more than the average for all levels of education ($31 757), so (2) is incorrect. People with a high school graduation certificate and/or some postsecondary education ($25 477) earn less on average than people with trades certificates or diplomas ($32 743), so (4) is incorrect. People with university certificates, diplomas, or degrees earn about 1.5 times as much on average as people with trades certificates or diplomas ($48 648 ÷ $32 743 = 1.48). This makes (5) incorrect.

24. **(1)** By examining the table, we can see that people with a high school graduation certificate and/or some postsecondary education ($25 477) earn less than the average for all occupations ($31 757). The remaining groups listed in the table earn more than the average.

25. **(3)** The median is the middle income level. If you list the incomes for each family from the top down, the median income is the one at which half the families earn more and half the families earn less. (1 and 2) The definition of *average income* is "the total income earned divided by the number of families." (4) The income necessary to sustain an adequate lifestyle is referred to as the Low Income Cut Off (LICO). (5) Income after taxes is called disposable income.

26. **(5)** The last column of the table shows that the increase for lone-parent families whose children are all 18 years and over was 0.7 per cent. The figures for the other family types are (1) 2.9, (2) 5.8, (3) 3.5, and (4) 19.3 per cent.

27. **(1)** The median income for couples with no children was $5489 less than the median for all families in 1990 ($54 560 − $49 071). The figures for the other family types were (2) $7766 more, (3) $23 250 more, (4) $29 763 less, and (5) $11 653 less.

28. **(5)** Germany (at $608 billion) is the second-largest exporter after the United States. (1) The United States has the highest GDP per capita. (2) China has the largest population. (3) The United States is the largest exporter. (4) Canada has the smallest population.

29. **(1)** 32 million ÷ 83 million = 0.38. (2) 1284 million ÷ 281 million = 4.5. (3) $26 600 ÷ $4 600 = 5.78. (4) $286 billion ÷ $312 billion = 0.917. (5) $261 billion ÷ $723 billion = 0.43.

30. **(1)** GDP per capita is one of the accepted economic figures to compare relative standards of living because it includes all (gross) goods and services produced by a nation. (2) Dividing annual exports by population does not give information on standard of living. (3) Annual exports alone do not show a relationship to the number of people who share those sales. (4) Dividing annual exports by GDP per capita compares an individual figure (per capita) with a total national figure. (5) Multiplying GDP per capita by population results in the GDP of a country and does not relate directly to individuals.

31. **(5)** The passage is citing the worldwide spread of the bicameral legislature as evidence that it is widely considered an effective form of government. (1) Therefore, the passage never implies that bicameral legislatures are not effective. (2 and 3) There is also no indication that this form is ancient or that it loses its effectiveness over a given period of time. (4) The passage certainly does not appear to criticize Canada for its choice of legislature, despite its global popularity.

32. **(4)** Both the Cabinet (which consists of the prime minister and cabinet ministers) and the House of Commons must approve a bill before it passes to the Senate, not just one or the other. (1 and 5) Her Majesty the Queen is not involved in this particular political process.

33. **(3)** The House of Commons is certainly in opposition to the more conservative Senate, "the place of 'sober second thought.'" The Liberal Party may indeed have the majority in the House of Commons, but this is not always the case, and it is never the case that they are the *only* party in the House (1). Nothing is mentioned in the passage about the House of Commons being lawless or disorganized (2), nor that liberalism controls the House in any way (4). Liberalism (not the Liberal Party) is certainly not as prevalent in the Senate as in the House; liberalism as an opposition to the Senate is mentioned in the passage (5).

34. **(5)** The cartoon depicts President George W. Bush, who ordered U.S. troops into Iraq, causing a dispute with France and Germany. (1) Canada is not represented in the cartoon. (2 and 3) Gerhard Schroeder was the chancellor of Germany and Jacques Chirac the president of France when the war in Iraq started; they are represented in the two figures on the right. (4) Britain is not represented in the cartoon.

35. **(3)** On the left side of the card is the statement that polls are open September 20, 22, 23, 24, 25, and 26, 2003. This is a total of six days. All other answers are therefore wrong.

36. **(2)** The wheelchair signs in the top centre of the card show that special facilities are available at 23 Brock Road South, and at 30 Minto Road. The other answers can all be verified from the card in the following places: (1) top left, (3) centre left, (4) upper left corner, (5) top right and bottom right.

37. **(4)** A bill must normally have the approval of the Cabinet before it is sent to (3) the House of Commons. This is the first stage in the normal passage of a bill. (2) The bill then goes to the Senate. (1) The governor-general sees the bill after the Senate. (5) Parliament comprises the House of Commons and the Senate, and does not represent a separate stage in the passage of a bill.

38. **(2)** The Conservatives won more seats than any other party (124) and therefore formed the government. Answers (1), (3), (4), and (5) are wrong because these parties all won fewer seats than the Conservatives did.

39. **(1)** The Bloc Québécois won 4.9 seats for every 1 percent share of the popular vote it gathered (51 seats divided by 10.5 percent share of the popular vote = 4.86). The other parties received fewer seats for every 1 percent of the popular vote they gathered. The figures are: (2) Conservatives 3.4; (3) Independents 1.0; (4) Liberals 3.4; (5) New Democratic Party 1.7.

40. **(4)** After five steps of Malthus's sequence, there would be six units of food for

32 members of the population. This amount ($^6/_{32}$ units) of food is less than one-quarter of the food available at the beginning of the sequence. (1 and 5) There will not be more food available in the future. (2 and 3) Food supply and population growth will not keep pace with each other.

41. **(4)** The problem Malthus identified is the inability of food supply to keep up with population growth; limiting families to one child would slow population growth, thus reducing the problem. (1 and 2) These choices would have the effect of increasing births and therefore population growth. (3) Bad harvests would reduce the availability of food and make it more difficult to feed the existing population. (5) If people lived longer, the death rate would decrease and population would increase.

42. **(3)** Fredericton experiences about 90 mm of precipitation in July. (1) Vancouver experiences 38 mm; (2) St. John's, 83 mm; (4) Winnipeg, 83 mm; and (5) Regina, 60 mm.

43. **(4)** Winnipeg is the coldest at $-18°C$. (1) Vancouver is $5°C$; (2) St. John's, $-2°C$; (3) Fredericton, $-10°C$; and (5) Regina, $-13°C$.

44. **(1)** You can tell from the climate graph that the temperature range for Vancouver—from January ($5°C$) to July ($25°C$)—is smaller than for any other city, suggesting that ocean waters have a warming influence in winter and a cooling effect in summer.

45. **(5)** This answer is correct because it specifies what is being measured in graph, where, and during what period. Titles of graphs and other figures should be as specific as possible. (1 and 2) These titles are not complete

enough; each is only a partial description. (3) This title is not accurate because the graph contains data for 2001, which is in the 21st century. (4) This title is a poor choice because the graph shows percentages, not growth.

46. **(3)** The graph tells us only about rural and urban populations by percentages. It tells us nothing about the ethnic makeup of the population. (1 and 5) These developments are consistent with the increasing urbanization of the population. (2 and 4) These developments are consistent with the decreasing rural nature of Canadian life.

47. **(2)** In the first 1500 years of the Common Era, world population increased 47 per cent, whereas in the two 100-year periods between 1800 and 2000, the increases were 100 per cent and 275 per cent, respectively. (1) The fastest increase took place between 1950 and 2000. (3) The population in 2000 was $6000 \div 300$, or 20 times the population in 1 c.e. (4) The period 1950–2000 saw the fastest population growth rate ever. (5) The slowest growth rate took place between 1 c.e. and 1000 (40 million in 1000 years).

48. **(3)** Low-income agricultural nations tend to be characterized by (among other things) high fertility rates. At 6.08, country C had the highest fertility rate of those listed. Notice that although the fertility rate is predicted to fall the most in country C and it is predicted to rise in country A (1) and country D (4), in 2050 it will still be highest in country C. In country B (2) and country E (5) the fertility rate is predicted to decline further and to remain below that of country C in 2050.

49. **(2)** India's population is predicted to grow by 322 million ($1363 - 1041 = 322$).

The figures (in millions) for the other choices are as follows: (1) China: $1431 - 1279 = 152$; (3) United States: $346 - 289 = 57$; (4) Indonesia: $272 - 214 = 58$; (5) Pakistan: $252 - 149 = 103$.

50. **(3)** The United States is considered a developed, industrial nation because it has a highly developed industrial economy, with a large part of its income coming from the service sector and high living standards for the average inhabitant. The other countries are considered developing nations. Although their economies are becoming more industrialized, a large part of their revenues are from the agricultural and manufacturing sectors, and average living standards are low.

GED Social Studies

Canadian History

CANADIAN HISTORY

ANCIENT CANADA

In the beginning the land was covered by immense glaciers. About a million years ago the advance and retreat of successive ice ages carved out large troughs that eventually became lakes, rivers, and valleys. Like giant sculptors, the glaciers levelled, pushed, and ground the earth as they shaped future land formations.

About 20 000 years ago the climate grew warmer and the glaciers retreated. Some parts were completely covered by vast inland seas, while others emerged as land. Between Siberia and Alaska a land bridge about 50 miles wide came into existence. With time the ancestors of Canada's Indians and Eskimos made their way across the land bridge in search of food and shelter. From Alaska these wandering peoples migrated eastward and southward by river valleys. Where conditions were favorable, small groups settled and flourished, but in isolation from one another. As a result, dozens of distinct native languages and ways of life emerged.

From the Beothuks, Micmac, and Maliseet on the eastern coast to the Kwakiutl, Haida, and Tsimshian of the Pacific Coast, each group of ancient peoples developed unique legends and heroes, leaders, and lifestyles. (The word *Canada*, in fact, comes from the Indian word *canata*, meaning "huts.") Modern archaeologists have determined much about these ancient peoples by studying artifacts such as pieces of pottery, arrowheads, and bones.

Questions

The following questions refer to the preceding passage. Read each question and choose the correct answer.

1. Canada's land formations were the result of huge

   (1) earthquakes.

   (2) glaciers.

   (3) tidal waves.

   (4) tornadoes.

   (5) volcanoes.

2. The first inhabitants of Canada were migrants from the continent of

   (1) Australia.

   (2) Asia.

   (3) Africa.

   (4) North America.

   (5) South America.

3. The native cultures that developed in Canada were located in

(1) the eastern part of the country.

(2) the central part of the country.

(3) the western part of the country.

(4) the northern part of the country.

(5) every part of the country.

Answers

1. (2)

2. (2)

3. (5)

CANADA'S PATH TO A CONSTITUTIONAL GOVERNMENT, 1763–1867

Between 1763 and 1867 the British government applied five documents to define Canada's government. The variety of documents was necessary to deal with the changing situation in North America during that period. The details of the five documents are summarized in Table 1.

Reactions to these documents varied. The French Canadians wanted things to remain largely the same as under the French regime. This meant that they wanted French institutions to remain in place, resisting English replacements for these institutions. The Roman Catholic clergy wanted to retain the preeminent position of their Church, and were generally opposed to special privileges for any other Church.

But there was another important group to be considered. Thousands of Americans opposed to the American Revolution came to Quebec to retain their British connections. Known as Tories (or traitors) in the United States, Canadians call them United Empire Loyalists—or Loyalists in short form. The Loyalists liked the British connection, but they also valued American democratic principles. They were shocked to find that there was no elected legislature in Quebec under the terms of the Proclamation (1763) and the Quebec Act (1774). They quickly pressed the British government to introduce an elected legislature. Recognizing that the Loyalists could be a valuable ally in future disputes with the United States, the British government responded to their concerns in the Constitution Act (1791).

Questions

The following questions refer to the preceding passage and to Table 1. Read each question and choose the correct answer.

1. With which document would the French Canadians have been most unhappy?

(1) Royal Proclamation of 1763

(2) Quebec Act of 1774

(3) Constitution Act of 1791

(4) Union Act of 1841

(5) Constitution Act of 1867

2. Which group of people would have been most supportive of the changes brought about by the Constitution Act of 1791?

(1) Roman Catholic clergy

(2) Small-town and village craftspeople

(3) Loyalist immigrants from the United States

(4) Leaders of French Canadian society, such as the *seigneurs*

(5) United States government

Table 1. Documents That Defined Canadian Government, 1763–1867

Document (date enacted)	Applicable territory	Major provisions
Royal Proclamation (1763)	Britain took over all the French territory in North America (acquiring ownership of all of eastern North America, from Newfoundland to Georgia and inland to the Great Lakes)	Canadian colonies under direct rule from London British civil and criminal law applied Protestant Church recognized
Quebec Act (1774)	All the British territory from modern eastern Quebec through the Great Lakes to the Ohio Valley (including parts of modern Ohio, Michigan, and Indiana)	Governor authorized to appoint a council of 18 to 23 advisors Governor authorized to issue laws Roman Catholic Church recognized French land and civil law, British criminal law applied
Constitution Act (1791)	Quebec divided at Ottawa River into Upper and Lower Canada; U.S. claim to the Ohio Valley territory recognized	Elected legislatures established in both Upper and Lower Canada French civil and land law applied in Lower Canada; British civil and land law applied in Upper Canada Roman Catholic Church recognized in Lower Canada; land grants to Protestant Church in Upper Canada
Union Act (1841)	Upper and Lower Canada renamed Canada West and Canada East	Legislatures of two Canadas joined, with each receiving 65 seats in the new legislature Legal differences between Canadas remained
Constitution Act (1867); originally called the British North America Act	Nova Scotia, New Brunswick, Quebec, Ontario	Federal system of national government established in Ottawa; provincial governments established French and English recognized as languages of Parliament French land and civil law applied in Quebec; British land law applied in other provinces; British criminal law applied everywhere

3. What external event would have made the plan to unite the colonies of British North America in 1867 more urgent?

(1) End of the Spanish-American War

(2) End of the War of 1812

(3) End of the First World War

(4) End of the Boer (or South African) War

(5) End of the American Civil War

Answers

1. (1)

2. (3)

3. (5)

THE AGE OF MACDONALD (1867–1891)

The prime minister of the new country was Sir John A. Macdonald. A masterful politician and one of the Fathers of Confederation, Macdonald was given the responsibility of guiding Canada through its formative years. He recognized that the new country's future depended on populating the vast western territory. In 1869 Canada purchased the Northwest Territories from the Hudson's Bay Company, and in 1870 Manitoba became the fifth province. In 1871 British Columbia joined with the promise that Canada would build a railway to the Pacific. In 1873 Prince Edward Island became the seventh province.

The building of a Pacific railway was a priority for Macdonald. He was not ignorant of the American desire to annex the Northwest Territories, however, and the construction costs were so enormous that Macdonald had to nego-tiate with several groups, including the Canada Pacific Railway Company. In 1873 it became known that the company had given money to the Conservatives during the 1872 election campaign. The resulting Pacific Scandal forced Macdonald to resign from office. For the next five years he remained out of power while the Liberal government of Alexander Mackenzie attempted to construct the railway in a piece-meal manner.

When Macdonald returned to power in 1878, the railway project had assumed a new urgency. British Columbia, frustrated with the delays, was threatening secession. Further, the American Northern Pacific Railway had resumed construction and would soon reach the Pacific Coast. Fortunately, in 1880 the prime minister found a new syndicate to build the rail line. Despite incredible difficulties, the line reached the Pacific in November 1885.

The first plank of Macdonald's National Policy was now complete. The second was protective tariffs to encourage a domestic manufacturing industry. The third was the settlement of the West—the issue that caused the old problems of language and religion to return with a vengeance.

When the Hudson's Bay Company had transferred its vast territory of the Northwest to Canada, no steps were taken to inform the people of Red River. More than half of them were French-speaking Métis, who were Roman Catholics. They feared being submerged by an influx of English-speaking Protestants. Anxious to protect their lands, language, and religion, they turned to Louis Riel for leadership. On November 2, 1869, Riel seized Fort Garry and established a provisional government, with himself as head. When the Canadian government responded by sending an army west to put down the rebellion, Riel fled to the United States.

In 1885 the Métis' grievances caused Riel to return. He proclaimed a provisional government in March 1885, but it was short lived. Riel was executed at Regina in November, causing a split in the country between English-speaking Protestants who clamoured for his death and French-speaking Catholics who had asked for clemency.

Sir John A. Macdonald died in 1891. He was one of Canada's outstanding prime ministers. Under his leadership the country expanded from four provinces to seven and was linked together by a transcontinental railway. He was able to build support in Quebec by forming a strong alliance with George Etienne Cartier. In so doing he established an important precedent for future Canadian politicians.

Questions

The following questions refer to the preceding passage. Read each question and choose the correct answer.

1. When Canada became a country, its first prime minister was

    (1) Alexander Mackenzie.

    (2) John A. Macdonald.

    (3) William Lyon Mackenzie.

    (4) Louis Joseph Paineau.

    (5) George Brown.

2. By 1873 Canada consisted of how many provinces?

    (1) Four

    (2) Five

    (3) Six

    (4) Seven

    (5) Eight

3. Which one of the following statements would not be an example of the National Policy initiated by McDonald?

    (1) Canada's prosperity lies in the export of its raw materials.

    (2) The country needs new settlers to populate the West.

    (3) Protective tariffs are necessary to encourage domestic manufacturing.

    (4) The undeveloped parts of the country need to be opened up and settled.

    (5) A railway is necessary to join the West to the rest of Canada.

4. One of the conclusions we can draw from the preceding passage is that

    (1) the Canadian government was concerned about what would happen to the Métis.

    (2) the Métis were a backward people who depended on the Canadian government for assistance.

    (3) the Métis' grievances were largely ignored by the Canadian government.

    (4) the Canadian government was determined to protect Métis lands, language, and religion.

    (5) only when Quebec complained did the Canadian government concern itself with the Métis.

5. Which one of the following statements would Macdonald have supported?

   (1) The concerns of Quebec are relatively unimportant and should be ignored.

   (2) The Province of Quebec should have more power in Confederation.

   (3) The Province of Quebec should have less power in Confederation.

   (4) As long as one of the major language groups is in control, Canada will be governed well.

   (5) The successful governing of Canada depends on an alliance between the leading figures of both language groups.

Answers

1. (2)

2. (4)

3. (1)

4. (3)

5. (5)

CANADA IN THE 20TH CENTURY

After Macdonald's death, four Conservative prime ministers followed in rapid succession. They proved incapable of handling the problems facing the country entering a new century. Thus, in 1896 Wilfrid Laurier led the Liberals to power and became Canada's first French Canadian prime minister.

The most serious problem facing Laurier concerned schools for French-speaking Catholics in Manitoba. Because of an influx of English-speaking settlers to the province, the French had become a minority. In 1890, the Manitoba government decided to stop paying for their education. French Canadians were incensed, and the Conservative Party was defeated in the 1896 election over the Manitoba Schools Question. Laurier's "answer" to the problem was to speak ambiguously about resolving it.

His "sunny ways" approach worked, and he remained in power for 15 years. His government encouraged massive emigration to the West, and as a result, the new provinces of Alberta and Saskatchewan were created in 1905. By 1911, however, Laurier was tired and his policies were unpopular. He fought the election on support of free trade with the United States but was defeated. A Conservative government under Robert Borden assumed power.

On August 4, 1914, events in Europe pulled Canada into the First World War. Germany's invasion of neutral Belgium led to Britain declaring war. As part of the British Empire, Canada had to join too. During the next four years more than 60 000 Canadians lost their lives in the war.

At home women assumed new roles in business and industry to replace men who had joined the army. As the war dragged on, volunteers for the military dropped off, leading the government to introduce conscription in 1917. Every eligible young man had to join the army. Although many English Canadians were opposed to conscription, primary opposition came from French Canadians. Riots broke out in Montreal, and English-Canadian newspapers accused Quebec of treason.

The postwar years were hard for many Canadians. Returning soldiers discovered that there were no jobs. Wages declined but prices continued to rise. As a result, many workers joined unions to demand better working conditions and pay. The Winnipeg General Strike in 1919 and the Cape Breton coal-mining strikes in the 1920s reflected the general discontent. Yet by the end of the decade, prosperity had returned, and Canadians were hopeful for the future. The crash of the stock market on October 29, 1929, erased these hopes.

The Great Depression lasted 10 years and caused untold damage, economically and socially. Many lost faith in the old political parties and turned to the new ones, such as the Co-operative Commonwealth Federation (CCF). Some provinces elected new leaders who promised economic solutions. Renewed prosperity was to come from another source, however.

On September 10, 1939, Canada went to war on Britain's side against Germany. For the next five years Canadians experienced many of the same hardships of the previous war. Conscription was again a divisive issue. Yet the Second World War had some beneficial consequences as well. At the insistence of the CCF, the government introduced several social programs, such as Unemployment Insurance (1940) and the Family Allowance (1944).

At the war's end, Europe was largely destroyed, and the Soviet Union and communism replaced Germany and Naziism as the enemy. On April 4, 1949, Canada and 15 other western countries signed the North Atlantic Treaty, forming the North Atlantic Treaty Organization (NATO). With this alliance the member countries promised to consider an attack on any one of them as an attack on them all. In 1957 the Soviet Union's launching of the *Sputnik* satellite and its development of atom and hydrogen bombs led to the formation of the North American Aerospace Defense Command (NORAD) through an agreement between Canada and the United States signed in 1958.

Canada's role in world affairs was also seen in the Commonwealth. In the postwar period Canada played a leading role in keeping former colonies—now new countries—within the Commonwealth. By so doing, it transformed the Commonwealth into a multiracial association.

Questions

The following questions refer to the preceding passage. Read each question and choose the correct answer.

1. The Manitoba Schools Question arose over the issue of the provincial government

    (1) expanding French-language education.

    (2) refusing to continue paying for French-language education.

    (3) supporting neither French- nor English-language education.

    (4) expanding English-language education.

    (5) decreasing French-language education.

2. Because of Prime Minister Laurier's encouragement of immigration, two new provinces came into being in 1905. They were

    (1) New Brunswick and Prince Edward Island.

    (2) Manitoba and Saskatchewan.

    (3) Saskatchewan and Alberta.

    (4) Alberta and British Columbia.

    (5) Yukon and the Northwest Territories.

3. One conclusion that can be drawn from the preceding passage is that Canada

    (1) played an important role in the First World War.

    (2) played a minor role in the First World War.

    (3) played no role in the First World War.

    (4) entered the war unwillingly.

    (5) entered the war but without reason.

4. The issue that divided English Canadians and French Canadians during the First World War was

    (1) food shortages.

    (2) rationing.

    (3) women working.

    (4) conscription.

    (5) the loss of life.

5. Which one of the following was **not** evidence of people's discontent during the Depression?

    (1) New leaders were elected in some provinces.

    (2) The CCF, a new political party, was founded.

    (3) The old political parties were unpopular.

    (4) The Depression caused great economic and social damage.

    (5) People lost faith in the old political leaders.

6. One of the conclusions that can be drawn from this passage is that

    (1) the end of the Second World War brought peace and stability to the world.

    (2) the communist threat forced new alliances and agreements among the nations of the world.

    (3) more countries withdrew from international alliances and concerned themselves with domestic problems.

    (4) a new era of friendship with the Soviet Union began.

    (5) attention shifted from Europe to Africa.

Answers

1. (2)
2. (3)
3. (1)
4. (4)
5. (4)
6. (2)

Table 2. Canadian Government Finances, 1911–1925 (Canadian dollars in millions)

Year	Expenditures				Revenue	National debt
	Defence	Transportation	Veterans*	Total		
1911	9.7	62.6	0.1	136.0	136.1	462.5
1914	72.4	78.5	0.7	246.4	133.0	749.7
1915	172.5	84.5	0.8	337.9	172.1	973.9
1916	312.0	68.5	3.8	496.7	232.7	1409.9
1917	343.8	93.9	8.2	573.5	260.8	1870.9
1918	438.7	86.2	30.3	695.6	312.9	2638.2
1919	346.6	61.4	74.6	740.1	349.7	2978.4
1925	14.1	74.2	46.1	355.6	383.3	3240.1

*Refers to benefits for veterans and survivors.

THE FIRST WORLD WAR (1914–1918) AND CANADA'S FINANCES

Canada fought beside Britain and France against Germany in the First World War. Some 620 000 Canadians enlisted in the military forces, and 61 000 were killed or went missing. It was an enormous contribution to the victorious side. Moreover, Canada made a significant financial contribution to the European war. Table 2 summarizes the federal government's finances during that period.

Questions

The following questions refer to the preceding passage and Table 2. Read each question and choose the correct answer.

1. According to Table 2, which item rose the most between 1911 and 1925?

    (1) Defence

    (2) Transportation

    (3) Total expenditures

    (4) Revenue

    (5) National debt

2. What would you normally expect a government to do to try to permanently reduce a steady growth in the national debt?

    (1) Lower taxes

    (2) Raise expenditures

    (3) Raise taxes

    (4) Borrow more money

    (5) Print more currency

Answers

1. (5)

2. (3)

CHALLENGES OF THE POST–WORLD WAR II PERIOD, 1945–1976

After the Second World War, increased population and industrial growth made road transportation important. In 1949, with passage of the Trans-Canada Highway Act, the Canadian government agreed to pay half the cost of road construction. By 1962 the 4860-mile intercontinental road from Victoria, British Columbia, to St. John's, Newfoundland, was officially open.

Another significant transportation project in the 1950s was the construction of the St. Lawrence Seaway. Completed in 1959, the seaway was a joint Canada–U.S. venture that permitted oceangoing ships to travel to the Great Lakes. Canada's industries and overseas trade were stimulated as a result.

The postwar period was marked by the expansion of television into most Canadian homes. This proved to be a mixed blessing. The spread of cable TV has contributed to the Americanization of Canada and thus has threatened Canadian culture. As a result, the Canadian Radio-Television and Telecommunications Commission (CRTC) was established in 1968 to ensure a high proportion of Canadian content on radio and television.

From 1939 to 1945 Ottawa had assumed wide powers to meet the demands of a country involved in total war. When the war ended, the provinces hoped to recover their former powers. As a result, federal-provincial conferences were developed as a means of coordinating the efforts of both levels of government. As Canada approached its centennial, however, the relationship between Ottawa and the provinces was becoming increasingly strained. The issue that almost brought it to the breaking point was that of language.

In 1960 a new government was elected in Quebec. It began an era of change known as the Quiet Revolution. It sprang from the determination of Quebeckers not to be swallowed up by the English-speaking majority around them. They gave notice that they—not Ottawans—were going to run their own affairs.

During the 1960s and 1970s the struggle between Ottawa and Quebec continued, particularly over recognition of French as Quebec's primary language. Some Quebeckers were convinced that only as an independent state would French Canadians enjoy the rights and power they desired.

The nationalism generated during this time led to the emergence of separatist parties, each advocating a different course of action. The most extreme was the Front de Libération du Québec (FLQ). A secretive organization committed to violence in achieving its ends, the FLQ set off several bombs in Montreal. In 1970 they kidnapped a British diplomat, James Cross, and a Quebec cabinet minister, Pierre Laporte. The federal government introduced emergency measures to deal with the situation, and several hundred Quebeckers were arrested and questioned.

The peaceful alternative to separatism was represented by the Parti Québécois (PQ) and its leader, René Lévesque. In 1976 the PQ came to power, and in 1980 a referendum on sovereignty was held in Quebec. It was defeated. Since then the federal government and provinces have attempted to work out new constitutional arrangements that would recognize Quebec as a "distinct society." These efforts have largely met with failure. As a result, Quebec's position in Canada will continue to be debated for some time.

Canadian dependence on the United States for continental defence was a fact of postwar life. Yet growing awareness of the extent of American ownership and control of Canada's industries led to concern and resentment among some Canadians. The economic relationship of the two countries has often been an unsettled one, but their proximity has been advantageous to both. The passage of the Free Trade Agreement (FTA) by Canada and the United States is proof that economic ties will continue to remain close.

As one of the founding members of the United Nations in 1945, Canada has always been committed to the maintenance of world peace. It was a Canadian, Lester Pearson, who was responsible for the idea of a United Nations peacekeeping force. Canadian service personnel have participated in peacekeeping operations in the Middle East, Africa, South Asia, Latin America, and Europe.

In recent years Canadians have come to realize that an action or event in any one country, such as the collapse of the Soviet Union, often has an international impact. Nuclear waste, pollution, and the depletion of the ozone layer and rain forests are problems that affect everyone. As a result, Greenpeace was founded in British Columbia. Through its protest actions around the world, the organization has defended the environment.

Electronics, supersonic jets, and communication satellites have made Canadians part of the "global village." Unlike John Cabot and Jacques Cartier, whose world was narrow and restricted, modern Canadians have a world within easy reach. Canada has truly become part of the world community.

Questions

The following questions refer to the preceding passage. Read each question and choose the correct answer.

1. Canada has faced several challenges in the modern world. Which one of the following is **not** one of these challenges?

    (1) Construction of railroads

    (2) The Americanization of Canada through television

    (3) Threats to the environment

    (4) American control of Canadian industries

    (5) Federal-provincial relations

2. The intercontinental road, which opened in 1962 to link Newfoundland with British Columbia, was the

    (1) St. Lawrence Seaway.

    (2) Trans-National Highway.

    (3) St. Lawrence Highway.

    (4) Trans-Canada Highway.

    (5) Trans-Canada Seaway.

3. The period of change that swept through Quebec in the 1960s was called the

    (1) Unquiet Revolution.

    (2) Quiet Revolution.

    (3) period of unrest.

    (4) time of troubles.

    (5) Canadian Revolution.

4. The governing political party in Quebec that held a referendum on sovereignty in 1980 was the

    (1) Front de Libération du Québec.

    (2) Parti Française.

    (3) Parti Nationale.

    (4) FLQ.

    (5) Parti Québécois.

5. One conclusion that can be drawn from this passage is that

    (1) Canadians are committed to maintaining peace in the world.

    (2) Canadian leadership on world issues is sadly lacking.

    (3) Canadians are not concerned about environmental issues.

    (4) Modern technology plays a relatively minor role in Canadian life.

    (5) Canada's primary concern is with events happening within its borders.

Answers

1. (1)

2. (4)

3. (2)

4. (5)

5. (1)

FAILURE OF THE MEECH LAKE ACCORD, 1987–1990

In 1987 Prime Minister Brian Mulroney reached an agreement with all the provincial premiers in an attempt to get Quebec to sign the new constitutional arrangements that had been adopted in 1982. Because the agreement was signed at the prime minister's official summer residence at Meech Lake, in the Gatineau Hills of Quebec, it was called the Meech Lake Accord. Under the terms of the agreement, it would become law if Parliament and all 10 provincial legislatures accepted it during the next three years.

The Meech Lake Accord recognized "within Canada, the distinct identity of Quebec." It guaranteed that three of the nine judges of the Supreme Court of Canada would come from the courts of Quebec, and it allowed the government of Quebec a greater role in deciding who could immigrate to that province. But the Meech Lake Accord ultimately failed when the Manitoba and Newfoundland legislatures did not accept it before the three-year deadline expired. There was much blaming among the federal and provincial governments over the accord's failure. Some provinces felt they did not get enough out of the accord. Although every province would get a veto on future constitutional reform, the accord failed to include reform of the Senate, which some western provinces favoured. Others felt that they had had their arms twisted by the federal government to accept what was simply a bad agreement. Amid the bickering that followed, the cartoon shown in Figure 1 was published. Prime Minister Mulroney is pictured in the boat along with the Canadian beaver.

Figure 1.
Source: Malcolm Mayes/artizans.com.

Questions

The following questions refer to the preceding passage. Read each question and choose the correct answer.

1. Which of the following items was **not** part of the Meech Lake Accord?

    (1) Recognition of Quebec's distinct society

    (2) Senate reform

    (3) A new role for Quebec in selecting immigrants

    (4) Three Supreme Court judges coming from Quebec's courts

    (5) A veto for all provinces on future constitutional reform

2. What is the cartoonist saying about the Meech Lake Accord?

    (1) It was a good idea.

    (2) It would have brought calm to Canadian politics.

    (3) It was Mulroney's insistence that led Canada into a storm.

    (4) It was Mulroney's calm manner that helped Canada avoid a storm.

    (5) The Meech Lake Accord will be quickly forgotten.

Answers

1. (2)

2. (3)

CANADIAN CHARTER OF RIGHTS AND FREEDOMS

In 1982 the Canadian constitution was changed to remove all references to Britain as part of the Canadian government and court system. This process was called patriation of the Canadian constitution. All future aspects of the Canadian constitution, including the power to amend it, would be the responsibility of the Canadian government. Additionally, the 1982 constitution included the Canadian Charter of Rights and Freedoms. The Charter is the highest Canadian law, and federal and provincial laws must, in general, not contradict anything in it. If a law contradicts the Charter, a court can declare the law or any part of it invalid. This change made the Canadian political system more American by giving more powers of review to the courts and placing emphasis on individual, as opposed to collective, freedoms. Following are some extracts from the Charter.

Guarantee of Rights and Freedoms

1. The Canadian Charter of Rights and Freedoms guarantees the rights and freedoms set out in it subject only to such reasonable limits prescribed by law as can be demonstrably justified in a free and democratic society.

Fundamental Freedoms

2. Everyone has the following fundamental freedoms: (a) freedom of conscience and religion; (b) freedom of thought, belief, opinion, and expression, including freedom of the press and other media of communication; (c) freedom of peaceful assembly; and (d) freedom of association.

Equality Rights

15. Every individual is equal before the law and has the right to equal protection and equal benefit of the law without discrimination, and in particular, without discrimination based on race, national or ethnic origin, colour, religion, sex, age, or mental or physical disability.

Questions

The following questions refer to the preceding passage. Read each question and choose the correct answer.

1. If a law contradicts the Charter, who has the power to declare the law invalid?

    (1) Canadian federal government

    (2) A court

    (3) Voters

    (4) British government

    (5) United States government

2. What do you think Section 1 of the Charter means?

    (1) There are no limits to individual rights and freedoms.

    (2) In a free and democratic society, individual rights and freedoms do not need to be justified.

    (3) It is important to protest when we think our rights and freedoms have not been guaranteed in a free and democratic society.

    (4) Our rights and freedoms can be limited if this limitation can be shown to be reasonable for people living in a free and democratic society.

    (5) There are no limits in a free and democratic society that can be demonstrated as reasonable in restricting individual rights and freedoms.

3. In 1985, 11-year-old Justine Blainey took the Ontario Hockey Association to court when it tried to prevent her from playing for a boys' hockey team. (OHA rules required separate boys' and girls' teams and leagues.) In 1986 the Supreme Court of Canada ruled in Ms. Blainey's favour and ordered the OHA to change its rules to allow girls who qualify for a place on a boys' team to play for it. Which of Ms. Blainey's rights, guaranteed by the Charter, was the Supreme Court upholding?

    (1) Freedom of conscience and religion

    (2) Freedom of thought, opinion, belief, and expression

    (3) Freedom of peaceful assembly

    (4) Freedom of association

    (5) Equality rights

Answers

1. (2)

2. (4)

3. (5)

Table 3. Canadian Public Opinion about Participating in the Invasion of Iraq

Position	Percentage of decided people taking this position
Opposed to Canadian participation under any circumstances	18
In favour of Canadian participation under any circumstances	22
In favour only with United Nations approval	57
In favour only with United Nations approval but with additional reservations	3

CANADIAN FOREIGN POLICY IN THE 21ST CENTURY

Throughout the 20th century, Canada supported its traditional allies Britain and the United States in wars such as the First and Second World Wars (1914–1918 and 1939–1945, respectively), the Korean War (1950–1953), and the Gulf War (1990–1991). However, when the United States failed to win United Nations support for the invasion of Iraq, in 2002 Prime Minister Jean Chrétien announced that Canada would not send troops to assist. When the invasion took place in 2003, American, British, and Australian troops participated. After the fall of Saddam Hussein, troops from numerous other countries went to Iraq as peacekeepers, but no Canadians were among them. If these events are typical of a new Canadian foreign policy, they will mark a significant departure from the past. Table 3 summarizes Canadian public opinion on the Iraq war in late 2002.

1. Which of the following conclusions may be correctly drawn about the issue of possible Canadian participation in the invasion of Iraq?

   (1) Prime Minister Chrétien misjudged Canadian public opinion.

   (2) More people were opposed to Canadian participation under any circumstances than were in favour of it.

   (3) The Canadian government's position on the possibility of participation in the invasion of Iraq was consistent with its position on participation in the major wars of the 20th century.

   (4) Prime Minister Chrétien correctly judged Canadian public opinion.

   (5) Canada participated by sending troops for the invasion of Iraq in 2003.

Question

The following question refers to the preceding passage. Read the question and choose the correct answer.

Answers

1. (4)

GED Social Studies

Economics

ECONOMICS

NEEDS AND WANTS

People need certain basic goods to survive: a place to live, food to eat, and basic clothing to cover their bodies. Economists refer to these basics as **economic needs**. In addition, people desire various goods and services—such as televisions, microwave ovens, and vacations—that improve or enhance the quality of their lives. Economists refer to these nonessential items as **economic wants**. Economics is the study of the way people meet both their economic wants and their economic needs. In essence, **economics** is the study of the allocation of scarce resources.

Because people's economic needs and economic wants outstrip an economy's ability to supply them, goods and services become scarce. At any given time in an economy, relative to the resources necessary to produce goods and services, people's economic needs and wants will be greater than the available supply of goods and services. As incomes rise and new technology develops, the demand for new and different products increases. Unlimited economic needs and wants and relatively limited resources results in economic **scarcity**.

Resources can be allocated to only one good or service at a time. Therefore, people must make economic choices. The difference between the cost of one item and that of another is one way to define **opportunity cost**. What a buyer must give up to obtain a good is another expression of the opportunity cost. For example, if a government decides to sell parkland for a shopping mall development, the cost of the new shopping mall will be the loss of a park. And if a student spends money on a school trip rather than saving for postsecondary education, the opportunity cost of that trip can be expressed in terms of lost savings for future education.

Questions

The following questions refer to the preceding passage. Read each question and choose the correct answer.

1. Which one of the following would most economists consider an economic need?

   (1) Running shoes

   (2) Potato chips

   (3) Shelter

   (4) Vacation

   (5) Car

2. Which one of the following would most economists consider an economic want?

(1) MP3 player

(2) Basic food

(3) Clothing

(4) Shelter

(5) Basic health services

3. For his lunch Santo decides to buy a salad, which costs half as much as a small pizza. Identify the opportunity cost of the salad.

(1) One pizza

(2) Two pizzas

(3) Two salads

(4) One-half of a pizza

(5) One-half of a salad

4. Which of the following best explains why people must always make economic choices?

(1) Unlimited economic needs and wants

(2) Limited resources

(3) Relative limited resources

(4) Scarcity

(5) New technology

Answers

1. (3)

2. (1)

3. (4)

4. (4)

ECONOMIC SYSTEMS

In a **traditional economy** a small group or community makes all economic decisions based on custom or tradition. People produce goods in the same way that their ancestors did. Because the community or group owns all resources, no one person controls property or other resources; resources belong to the group. For example, for many North American Aborigines, land cannot be privately owned or claimed for settlement with written deeds; the land belongs to the people. Tradition and custom determine who does what type of work and how the community distributes the results of that work.

In a **planned economy** the government or state owns all or the majority of resources and decides how resources will be organized for production and what goods and services will be offered in the marketplace, at what price, and in what quantities. State planners also determine wage levels for workers. Price plays a minor role in determining the supply of goods and services; government often sets the prices for goods and services, and in many cases subsidizes items like food. Few people own private property. Since the late 1980s most planned economies have moved toward a market model.

In a **pure market economy** individuals determine their economic fate. They own resources that they can sell to producers for profit. Through the forces of supply and demand, the price and quantity of a good or service is determined. Consumers attempt to obtain the largest quantities of quality goods and services at the lowest prices, while producers seek the greatest profits. Producer demand and the supply of labour determine wages. Government intervenes in the economy in a limited way by providing essential services such as infrastructure.

In reality no pure market economies exist. Most so-called market economies reflect the characteristics of traditional, planned, and pure market economies. In a **mixed economy**, such as that of Canada or the United States, the government acts as a consumer, producer, regulator, and educator in the economy, while individuals, motivated by self-interest and profit, pursue their economic needs and wants in the marketplace.

Questions

The following questions refer to the preceding passage. Read each question and choose the correct answer.

1. Which of the following **best** reflects a traditional economy?

    (1) Private property

    (2) Five-year plans

    (3) Large-scale competition

    (4) Community ownership of resources

    (5) Government-established production quotas

2. Which of the following is characteristic of a planned economy?

    (1) Profit

    (2) Unchanged methods of production over a long period of time

    (3) State ownership of resources

    (4) Competition among producers

    (5) Subsidized food prices

3. Which of the following **best** reflects a market economy?

    (1) Custom determines occupation.

    (2) The government determines the use of resources.

    (3) Supply and demand determine the price and quantity of goods and services produced and consumed.

    (4) The community shares in the results of production.

    (5) The government establishes wage guidelines.

Answers

1. (4)

2. (3)

3. (3)

CIRCULAR FLOW OF ECONOMIC ACTIVITY

To illustrate the interaction among the various economic players in an economy, economists use a model known as the circular flow model. A simple **circular flow model** like Figure 1 shows two types of markets, factor markets and product markets, and two groups of decision makers, businesses and households. Economists assume, for the sake of simplicity, that households, often referred to as consumers, own all factors of production and that businesses, often referred to as producers, represent the main purchasers of resources.

In a **factor market** households sell factors of production: natural, human, and capital resources. **Natural resources** represent such things as oil, forests, minerals, and land. **Human resources** represent labour, entrepreneurship, and mental activity. **Capital resources** represent anything that aids in the production of a good or service. For example, economists consider a robot capital because it aids in the production of a product. Because money buys capital, economists often refer to money as **money capital**.

In a **product market** households exchange with businesses, paying for goods and services. Households attempt to obtain the greatest quantity of quality goods and services at the lowest prices, while businesses seek to sell the most goods and services for the greatest profit.

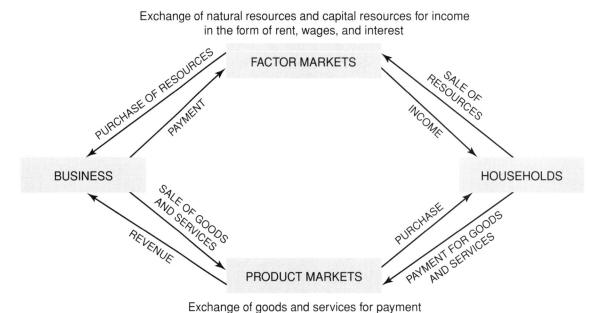

Exchange of natural resources and capital resources for income in the form of rent, wages, and interest

Exchange of goods and services for payment

Figure 1. Circular Flow Model

Questions

The following questions refer to the preceding passage and Figure 1. Read each question and choose the correct answer.

1. The circular flow model illustrates which of the following?

    (1) Actual human economic behaviour

    (2) Interaction of economic behaviours

    (3) Payment for goods

    (4) Payment for services

    (5) Payment for factors of production

2. Which of the following **best** describes the activity in the product market?

    (1) People pay for factors of production.

    (2) People pay for services.

    (3) People pay for goods.

    (4) People pay for natural resources.

    (5) People pay for goods and services.

Answers

1. (2)

2. (5)

COMPETITION

In pursuit of profits, producers in an economy compete in various ways. Depending on the number of producers and buyers, competition appears at four basic levels in most economies: pure monopoly, pure competition, oligopoly, and monopolistic competition.

Under a **pure monopoly**, one seller dominates the market of many buyers. Monopolies control both the supply of goods and services and their prices. Monopolies also erect barriers to other competitors in the market. Usually, a monopoly's product has few or no close substitutes. Provincial hydro companies represent a good example of a pure monopoly.

In a **pure competition** economy, many sellers and many buyers exchange goods and services that compete for a share of the market. Producers make similar products and have the freedom to enter or leave the marketplace; no barriers exist in a pure competition economy. As well-informed participants, both sellers and buyers freely exchange in the marketplace.

An **oligopoly** is similar to a monopoly, but instead of one supplier, a few work together to control a market. When few sellers control a market of many buyers, an oligopoly exists. The Organization of Petroleum Exporting Countries (OPEC) is an example of an oligopoly. With few companies making similar products, such as automobiles, little price competition exists.

When numerous sellers produce various products and compete through price and advertising, a **monopolistic competition** market exits. Producers can easily leave or enter this type of market. As a monopolistic competitor, the computer industry has a monopoly over the production and price of computers, but individual companies compete by pricing, service, and advertising.

Questions

The following questions refer to the preceding passage. Read each question and choose the correct answer.

1. Which of the following is an example of a monopoly?

    (1) In Canada, there are only two licensed satellite television program suppliers, who compete with each other for customers.

    (2) There are thousands of privately owned stores in Vancouver that compete with each other for a share of the market.

    (3) Until the 1990s in most of Ontario and Quebec, if you wanted telephone service, you had to buy the service from Bell Canada.

    (4) Air Canada has about 80 per cent of the domestic traffic in Canada, with the remainder being made up by Westjet and a few regional carriers.

    (5) There are many pharmaceutical companies producing medicines in Canada, but their prices are subject to regulation by the federal government.

2. Which of the following is the best example of pure competition?

    (1) In Canada, there are only two licensed satellite television program suppliers, who compete with each other for customers.

    (2) There are thousands of privately owned stores in Vancouver that compete with each other for a share of the market.

    (3) Until the 1990s in most of Ontario and Quebec, if you wanted telephone service, you had to buy the service from Bell Canada.

    (4) Air Canada has about 80 per cent of the domestic traffic in Canada, with the remainder being made up by Westjet and a few regional carriers.

    (5) There are many pharmaceutical companies producing medicines in Canada, but their prices are subject to regulation by the federal government.

3. Which of the following is being described in what follows?

    In a small and isolated Ontario town, there are two gas stations. Each is owned by a different large oil company. The two companies watch the price being charged at their competitor's station, and change their prices regularly to match each other. Just before each long weekend, both companies raise their prices when drivers are going longer distances. The two companies control the market because customers have nowhere else to buy gas.

    (1) Pure monopoly

    (2) Pure competition

    (3) Monopolistic competition

    (4) Oligopoly

    (5) None of the above

Answers

1. (3)

2. (2)

3. (3)

SUPPLY AND DEMAND

When people attempt to meet their economic needs and wants, they demand goods and services. All other things being equal, at lower prices, consumers demand more quantity of goods and services than at higher prices. Economists refer to this idea as **quantity demanded**; at any given price, consumers will demand a certain quantity of a good or service. The relationship between price and quantity is illustrated in Figure 2.

When consumers demand more or less of a good or service at each and every price, the entire demand curve shifts. A shift in demand differs from the quantity demanded in that the curve shifts up or down, while a change in the quantity demanded moves along the curve.

The factors influencing the shift in demand are income levels, personal taste, personal values, availability of substitutes or complementary goods or services, and consumer expectations about the future. For example, if the income level of a community increased by 50 per cent, consumers in that community would probably demand more goods and services at each price. Similarly, personal taste

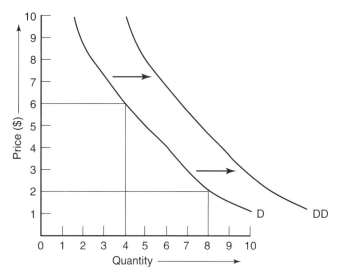

Figure 3. Shift in Demand

influences what and how much people buy, as do their values and attitudes. For instance, vegetarians certainly demand more nonmeat products than do nonvegetarians. Fluctuations in demand are depicted in Figure 3.

If people can substitute a cheaper product of similar quality, the demand for that product will probably increase. For example, many people use margarine as a butter substitute. Other products complement one another; when people purchase more Rollerblades, they will also purchase more of the accessories that relate to that product, such as kneepads and helmets.

In the pursuit of profits, producers will supply more goods and services at higher prices than at lower ones; at a given price, producers will supply a certain quantity of a good or service. Economists refer to this as **quantity supplied**, a move along the curve. Because producers seek to maximize their profits, they will supply more goods and services at higher prices. Figure 4 illustrates the concept of quantity supplied.

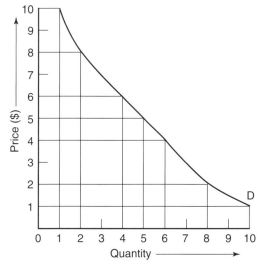

Figure 2. Quantity Demanded

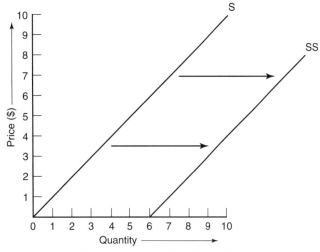

Figure 4. Quantity Supplied

A change in demand at each price results in a shift in the supply curve. Several factors cause a change in demand, among them price, new technology, production costs, and weather conditions. For example, if the price of carrots rose as a result of increased consumer demand, carrot producers would be willing to supply more carrots. If a hailstorm damaged almost 90 per cent of the Ontario peach crop, peach producers would offer fewer peaches at every price. Figure 5 illustrates supply shift.

Market price represents the price at which consumers are able and willing to buy a certain quantity of a good or service and producers are equally willing and able to supply that good or service. Only at market prices will the economic needs of both consumers and producers be met. Market price is illustrated in Figure 6.

Anything above market price will create a surplus of a good or service; producers will be willing to supply a certain quantity of the product, but consumers will be unwilling to buy it at that price. Similarly, anything below market price will result in a shortage of the good or service; consumers will be willing to buy more at the low price, but producers will be unwilling to supply the product.

A surplus (too much supplied) will drive prices down, while a shortage will push prices up. When there is no surplus or shortage, equilibrium is achieved.

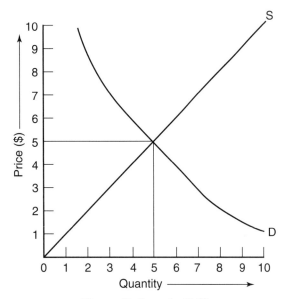

Figure 5. Supply Shift

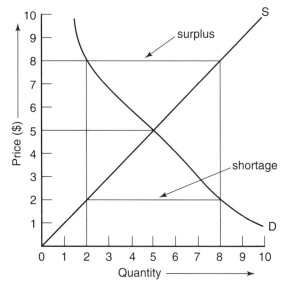

Figure 6. Market Price

Questions

The following questions refer to the preceding passage and figures. Read each question and choose the correct answer.

1. As price rises, the quantity demanded of a good or service

    (1) decreases.

    (2) increases.

    (3) remains the same.

    (4) increases and then decreases.

    (5) decreases and then increases.

2. A decrease in price causes

    (1) a shift in the supply curve to the left.

    (2) an increase in demand.

    (3) a shift in the supply curve to the right.

    (4) an increase in revenue.

    (5) no change in the supply curve.

3. The demand curve shows the relationship between

    (1) price and supply.

    (2) price and income.

    (3) price and values.

    (4) price and quantity demanded.

    (5) price and business revenue.

4. Which of the following factors **best** explains a decline in demand for beef products during the last 10 years?

    (1) Values

    (2) Income

    (3) Availability of substitute products

    (4) Availability of complementary goods

    (5) Price

5. A shift in the supply curve up and to the left means

    (1) producers are willing to supply more of a product.

    (2) producers are willing to supply less of a product at all prices.

    (3) producers are willing to supply the same quantity of a product.

    (4) at a specific price, producers are willing to supply more of a product.

    (5) at a specific price, producers are willing to supply less of a product.

6. A surplus exists in the marketplace when

    (1) demand exceeds supply.

    (2) supply equals demand.

    (3) demand equals supply.

    (4) price rises above market price.

    (5) price falls below market price.

Answers

1. (1)

The negative, downward-curving slope represents an inverse relationship, or movement in an opposite direction. Choice (2) describes a direct relationship, or a positive, upward-curving slope. Choice (3) describes a straight vertical line. Choices (4) and (5) may happen over time, but price would also have to go up and down.

2. (1)

A decrease in price would also lead to a decrease in quantity supplied, shifting the curve to the left. The curve is not describing demand. Choice (3) describes the opposite of what would happen. The curve in choice (4) provides no information about revenue. Choice (5) could not happen if there is a shift in price.

3. (4)

4. (1)

5. (2)

6. (4)

INFLATION

Inflation is a rise in the general level of prices. **Deflation** is a decline in the general level of prices. Figure 7 shows rates of inflation from 1980 to 1989.

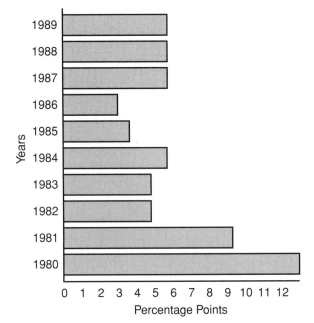

Figure 7. Inflation and Deflation

Banks have been deregulated since 1980, when the Depository Institutions Deregulation and Monetary Control Act was passed. Ceilings on interest rates were removed. The relationship between the rate of inflation and prices is illustrated in Figure 8.

Figure 8. Formula for Calculating Time Required for Prices to Double

Questions

The following questions refer to the preceding passage. Read each question and choose the correct answer.

Questions 1–3 refer to Figure 7.

1. Which three years had the same inflation rate?

    (1) 1988, 1989, 1980

    (2) 1981, 1985, 1987

    (3) 1987, 1988, 1989

    (4) 1986, 1981, 1980

    (5) 1980, 1985, 1988

2. Which year experienced the lowest inflation rate?

    (1) 1989

    (2) 1981

    (3) 1984

    (4) 1986

    (5) 1985

3. What year had the second-highest inflation rate?

    (1) 1984

    (2) 1989

    (3) 1986

    (4) 1980

    (5) 1981

Questions 4–6 refer to Table 1.

Table 1. Bank Failures

Year	Total bank failures
1980	10
1981	10
1982	42
1983	48
1984	79
1985	120
1986	138
1987	184
1988	200
1989	208

4. Based on the statistics shown in Table 1, the conclusion that can be drawn is

    (1) banks made riskier investments after 1980.

    (2) all banks were on sound financial footing.

    (3) there was a growth of banks.

    (4) all banks are covered by the Federal Deposit Insurance Corporation.

    (5) deregulation was a success.

5. The biggest jump in bank failures took place from

    (1) 1983 to 1984.

    (2) 1984 to 1985.

    (3) 1982 to 1983.

    (4) 1988 to 1989.

    (5) 1986 to 1987.

6. Which year had the fourth-highest number of bank failures?

    (1) 1988

    (2) 1982

    (3) 1986

    (4) 1983

    (5) 1987

Questions 7 and 8 refer to Figure 8.

7. If the inflation rate is 10 per cent, how many years will it take for prices to double?

    (1) 10 years

    (2) 20 years

    (3) 5 years

    (4) 7 years

    (5) 8 years

8. If the inflation rate is 7 per cent, how many years will it take for prices to double?

    (1) 5 years

    (2) 12 years

    (3) 7 years

    (4) 15 years

    (5) 10 years

Answers

1. (3)

2. (4)

3. (5)

4. (1)

5. (5)

6. (3)

7. (4)

8. (5)

FAMILY STRUCTURE AND MEDIAN INCOME

One of the things that economists do is to compare variables in one set of statistics with variables in another to see what relationships they can establish.

Family structure refers to the type of family being studied. For example, there are families headed by single (or "lone") parents and families headed by two parents (or "couples"). There are families with children and without. Economists also may classify families not only by the number of children but also by the age grouping(s) they fall into.

Imagine a computer-made list of the income that each family earned in one year. Imagine that the list shows the incomes in order from highest to lowest. If you go down the list exactly half way, you have come across the median income. Half of the families earn more than this amount, and half earn less.

You would reasonably expect two-parent families to have a higher median income than single-parent families. They have two people available to work for pay. (Not all two-parent families will choose for both parents to work, of course, but in a single-parent family this choice obviously does not exist.)

When economists compare family structure and median income, some interesting results emerge. The following table summarizes some of this information.

Table 2 summarizes earnings and family type in Canada in 2000. Median income is the income at which 50 per cent of families earned more and 50 per cent of families earned less.

Table 2. Family Type and Median Income before Taxes, 2000

Family type	Median income (in Canadian dollars)
All families	$55 016
Couple families with no children	$50 509
Couple families with at least one child under 18 years	$65 962
Couple families whose children are all 18 years and over	$80 545
Lone-parent families with at least one child under 18 years	$26 008
Lone-parent families whose children are all 18 years and over	$43 187

Question

The following question is based on Table 2. Read the question and choose the correct answer.

1. Which family type earned closest to the median income of all families in 2000?

    (1) Couple families with no children

    (2) Couple families with at least one child under 18 years

    (3) Couple families whose children are all 18 years and over

    (4) Lone-parent families with at least one child under 18 years

    (5) Lone-parent families whose children are all 18 years and over

Answer

1. (1)

ECONOMIC THEMES

The **labour force** includes employed workers and unemployed workers still seeking employment. When calculating the composition of the labour force, Statistics Canada excludes aboriginal people living on reserves, people under the age of 15, members of the armed forces, inmates and patients in prisons and psychiatric hospitals for more than six months, full-time students, residents of the Northwest Territories and the Yukon, and people no longer looking for work (often referred to as discouraged workers).

Numerous factors determine **wages**, including skill, education, risk, and experience. In general, people who have more skills, experience, and education and are willing to accept more risks earn higher wages than people without those characteristics.

Ultimately, however, wages will be determined by the supply of and demand for qualified workers. For example, at the end of the Gulf War of 1992, because of the large number of oil-well fires in the Gulf, the demand for skilled oil-well firefighters exceeded the supply. Consequently, the firefighters received higher salaries.

Among the factors influencing the demand for labour are seasons, technology, economic cycles, discrimination, and government programs. For example, people working in the fishing or farming industry will obtain more employment in certain seasons than in others, while people working in an industry that has been affected by changes in production, such as the introduction of robots, will experience increasing unemployment. Some people fail to obtain a job because of discrimination, while others gain employment as a result of government job-creation programs.

Each month Statistics Canada calculates unemployment through telephone surveys and information collected from its employment centers. Statistics Canada considers **unemployed workers** to be those still looking for work. Unemployed workers who no longer seek employment are referred to as **discouraged workers**.

To calculate the unemployment rate, Statistics Canada divides the number of unemployed by the labour force and multiplies that number by 100. The unemployment rate does not reflect the real level of unemployment because it does not include discouraged workers.

Unemployment takes four basic forms: seasonal, frictional, structural, and cyclical. **Seasonal** unemployment is unemployment caused by the fact that the Canadian climate prevents some workers—for example outdoor construction workers—from working year-round. Because of the nature of the industry they work in, fish and farm workers become unemployed in the off or slow seasons. Economists refer to unemployment that results when a person is between jobs as **frictional** unemployment. When changes in production, such as the introduction of a new technology, creates unemployment, economists refer to this as **structural** unemployment. When an economy moves into a recession, economists refer to the resulting unemployment as **cyclical** unemployment.

Questions

The following questions refer to Table 3. Read each question and choose the correct answer.

1. Which province has the highest percentage of jobs in the manufacturing sector?

    (1) Alberta

    (2) Quebec

    (3) Nova Scotia

    (4) New Brunswick

    (5) Newfoundland and Labrador

2. Which of the following people would be classified in Table 3 as employed in a primary industry?

    (1) A farmer who operates a dairy operation to provide milk to a cheese factory

    (2) A financial advisor who invests the money you received in a relative's will

    (3) A forklift operator who stacks lumber in a retail centre

    (4) A truck driver who delivers petroleum products to service stations

    (5) A drill operator who removes ore from a gold mine

Table 3. Percentage of Jobs in Selected Employment Sectors, 2001

Province	Primary	Manufacturing	Construction	Transport and utilities	Services
Alberta	10.1	8.0	7.7	6.3	52.4
Quebec	2.8	17.6	4.6	5.4	53.1
Nova Scotia	5.2	10.0	6.1	5.2	56.8
New Brunswick	5.6	12.6	6.4	6.5	53.4
Newfoundland and Labrador	6.7	10.3	6.4	5.9	52.7

3. Which of the following people would be classified in the Table 3 as employed in a service industry?

   (1) A farmer who operates a dairy operation to provide milk to a cheese factory

   (2) A financial advisor who invests the money you received in a relative's will

   (3) A forklift operator who stacks lumber in a retail centre

   (4) A truck driver who delivers petroleum products to service stations

   (5) A drill operator who removes ore from a gold mine

Answers

1. (2)

2. (1)

3. (2)

INTERNATIONAL TRADE STATISTICS

Figures 9–11 show trade statistics for five nations.

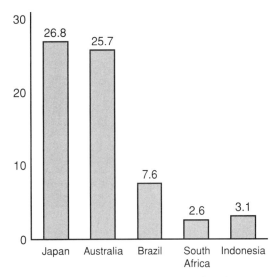

Figure 10. Gross Domestic Product (GDP) per Capita for Five Nations (in thousands of U.S. dollars)

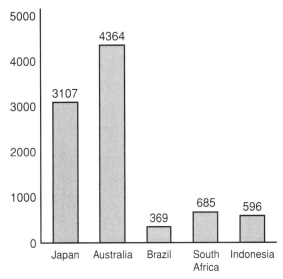

Figure 11. Exports per Capita for Five Nations (in U.S. dollars)

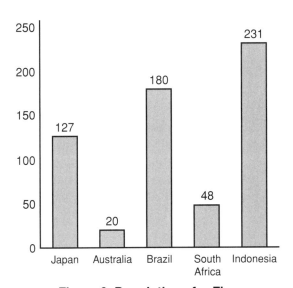

Figure 9. Populations for Five Nations (in millions)

Questions

The following questions refer to Figures 9–11. Read each question and choose the correct answer.

1. What is meant by the term *exports per capita*?

    (1) The goods and services a country brings in multiplied by its population

    (2) The goods and services a country sends out multiplied by its population

    (3) The goods and services a country sends out divided by its population

    (4) The goods and services a country brings in divided by its population

    (5) The goods and services a country sends out as a percentage of its population

2. Which statement can correctly be drawn from the figures?

    (1) The population of Australia is less than half that of South Africa.

    (2) The population of Indonesia is more than 12 times as large as that of Australia.

    (3) The GDP per capita of South Africa is less than half that of Indonesia.

    (4) The exports per capita of Japan are more than 100 times as great as those of Brazil.

    (5) The GDP per capita of Indonesia is more than seven times as great as its exports per capita.

3. Which conclusion can correctly be drawn from the graphs?

    (1) Countries with high populations tend to have lower GDP per capita figures.

    (2) Countries with high export per capita figures tend to have high GDP per capita figures.

    (3) Countries with low populations tend to have lower GDP per capita figures.

    (4) Countries with high export per capita figures tend to have low GDP per capita figures.

    (5) Countries with high export per capita figures tend to have high GDP per capita figures.

Answers

1. (3)

2. (1)

3. (2)

URBANISM AND GDP PER CAPITA

Ever since the industrial revolution of the 19th century, the populations of all developed nations have shifted from rural to urban settings. Manufacturing industries established themselves where there was already a good supply of labour (in towns and cities). This caused other people to migrate to towns and cities in search of steady work. As more nations have become developed, this rural to urban migration has been a feature of late-20th and early 21st-century history on a global scale. Mega cities—like Mexico City, Beijing, Hong Kong, New York, and Buenos Aires—dominate the regional economies of their nation. Canada is a good example of a country whose population has become increasingly urban over the course of the past century. Originally a nation of farms, villages, and small communities, by 2001 over 80 percent of its population lived in towns and cities.

In general, there is a link between highly urbanized nations and higher standards of living. Industries generate more wealth than agriculture. Industrial employees generally earn higher wages than those in agriculture. In the late 20th century, many developed nations experienced a shift from industrial to service industries. Many steel mills and manufacturing plants closed. New jobs arose in finance, insurance, call centres, and other service industries. But like their industrial predecessors, these service industries were generally urban-based. The link between city life and the possibility of high-paying jobs was preserved.

City dwellers can experience high crime rates, pollution, inferior housing, and other social ills. But cities also offer the chance of a better life for unemployed rural people. It is therefore likely that the worldwide growth of urbanism will continue for the foreseeable future.

Questions

The following questions refer to Table 4. Read each question and choose the correct answer.

Table 4. Percentage of Urbanized Population and GDP per Capita in Selected Countries, 2000

Country	Percentage of urbanized population	GDP per capita (in U.S. dollars)
Argentina	90%	$12 300
Australia	85%	$25 700
Poland	62%	$9100
Mexico	74%	$9000
Nigeria	36%	$900

1. What is meant by the term "Percentage of urbanized population"?

   (1) Percentage of the total population living in poverty

   (2) Percentage of the total population living in villages and country areas

   (3) Percentage of the total population living in towns and cities

   (4) Percentage of the total population with a high standard of living

   (5) Percentage of the total population with a low standard of living

2. Which of the following pairs appear to go together, based on the information in Table 4?

   (1) High urbanization and low GDP per capita

   (2) Medium urbanization and medium GDP per capita

   (3) Low urbanization and high GDP per capita

   (4) High urbanization and high GDP per capita

   (5) Low urbanization and medium GDP per capita

Answers

1. (3)
2. (4)

GED Social Studies

Civics and Government

CIVICS AND GOVERNMENT

NATURE OF POLITICAL SYSTEMS

Politics is the interaction of government and society. The goal of political power is to remain legitimate by resolving the natural conflict that pervades society. This conflict exists because of the many different cultures and ethnicities, demands, and desires of the people who live together in a particular society. As the ruling body of a society, government attempts to manage political conflict and allocate resources according to the values and diverse demands of society. A **government** is any ruling body that strives to make important decisions on behalf of a society. Underlying the people's agreement to abide by the decisions of a ruling body is a tacit agreement between the government and society: the government should act in the best interests of the people, and the people should respect the government's decisions. This concept is known as the **social contract**. A government is considered **legitimate** when it fulfills this basic contract.

A government's legitimacy is derived from its effective resolution of conflict and provides it with the right to exercise power. Legitimacy gives a government a certain range of power, known as **sovereignty**. Among the powers of a government are taxation and diplomatic representation. The latter power, for example, enables the government to make decisions regarding international affairs on behalf of the domestic society.

A **nation-state** is the most powerful form of political organization, as defined by the United Nations Charter. Canada is a nation-state. A **state** is a less powerful form of government that is able to enforce laws and maintain order, but only within a defined territory of a nation-state. A state is sovereign in some areas of jurisdiction, but not all. The boundary of sovereignty between a nation-state and a state is variable, depending on the form of government.

A **federation** is a nation-state that divides power among jurisdictions. The government of Canada is a federation that divides powers between provinces and the nation. A **unitary** system is one in which the national government holds authoritative power over all jurisdictions.

A **democracy** is a system of government in which the people of a society have the power of direct participation in a representative government. The primary way people can directly participate is by exercising their right to vote in open elections. With certain qualifications, virtually any person can also run for a political office. There are many ways for a society to participate in a democratic government. The word *democracy* comes from the Greek root words *demos* ("people") and *kratos* ("authority"). The power, sovereignty, and legitimacy of a democratic government are granted by the people. In his inaugural address, Abraham Lincoln defined the concept of democracy in this now-famous phrase: "of the people, by the people, for the people." Different democracies practice their powers in different ways because people around the world have different priorities. Canada is a democracy.

Questions

The following questions refer to the preceding passage. Read each question and choose the correct answer.

1. The nature of politics can best be described as

    (1) a means of acquiring power.

    (2) the interaction of government and society.

    (3) a government's right to exercise power.

    (4) the process of governmental decision making.

    (5) none of the above.

2. The basic principle of the social contract is

    (1) "a society must be united."

    (2) "a society must obey the government."

    (3) a legal document between government and society.

    (4) a tacit agreement between government and society.

    (5) "of the people, by the people, for the people."

3. The legitimacy of a government is derived from

    (1) the fulfillment of the social contract.

    (2) the sovereignty of a nation-state.

    (3) the division of power among jurisdictions.

    (4) the effective resolution of natural conflict in society.

    (5) both (1) and (4).

4. A legitimate government cannot

    (1) exercise a certain range of powers.

    (2) refute the social contract.

    (3) allocate resources.

    (4) divide power among jurisdictions.

    (5) choose its own form of political organization.

5. Canada is both

    (1) a state and a federation.

    (2) a nation-state and an autocracy.

    (3) a democracy and a state.

    (4) a democracy and a unitary system.

    (5) a democracy and a federation.

6. The most powerful form of political organization as defined by the United Nations Charter is

   (1) a state.

   (2) a federation.

   (3) a nation-state.

   (4) a nation.

   (5) a democracy.

7. A democracy gives the people the power to

   (1) tax.

   (2) vote.

   (3) run for a government office.

   (4) divide sovereignty.

   (5) both (2) and (3).

8. The government of Canada can do all the following **except**

   (1) assume authoritative power over all jurisdictions.

   (2) allow people to vote.

   (3) tax and assume diplomatic duties.

   (4) allocate national resources.

   (5) none of the above.

Answers

1. (2)

2. (4)

3. (5)

4. (2)

5. (5)

6. (3)

7. (5)

8. (1)

CANADIAN POLITICAL PROCESS

The access to political parties is one fundamental way in which the government gains its legitimacy and power in Canada. Citizens have the freedom to become involved in the political process by participating in political parties. These organizations develop the political fabric of the nation by familiarizing young leaders with the nation's political processes and encouraging them to become involved in political activities such as organizing campaigns for the electorate and canvassing for parliamentary candidates. Political parties provide stability by legitimizing those who have proven themselves to be capable of leading their country. The party elected into government provides a foundation for the executive branch, the legislature, and the Cabinet. The ruling party must bring together the needs of the people in and out of the party to represent its citizens as a government.

Canada has a multiparty system; however, only two parties have significantly ruled the government: the Progressive Conservatives and the Liberals. A third party sometimes establishes a power base that can balance power between the two major parties. The Social Credit and the New Democratic parties have been strong in that role. Other third parties have emerged without accumulating significant power.

The right to vote is essential to a democracy. Every Canadian citizen 18 years of age and older has the right to vote in an election. Qualified citizens also have the right to join or create a new political party. A citizen may also try to influence government policy in other ways. For example, "access points" enhance a citizen's ability to change the society. Access points are opportunities in which citizens can exert influence and express their ideas into laws and policies being formulated. Examples of such access points are individual members who may be on special parliamentary committees, members of a caucus, members of the Cabinet, a government bureaucracy, input on bills passed through Parliament, and informal meetings with high government officials. In special situations a royal commission is ordered to hear whatever Canadians may think on a particular issue. Reports are prepared for final policy considerations. A Canadian citizen's participation in government can run the gamut from a simple vote to complex activity in groups that influence government policy.

1. Political parties in Canada are
    (1) a way to become involved in the political process.
    (2) the only recourse to voting privileges.
    (3) the source of power for youth.
    (4) the only legitimizing factor of Canadian government.
    (5) none of the above.

2. The ruling party in Canada is
    (1) the Social Credit.
    (2) the New Democratic.
    (3) the Progressive Liberals.
    (4) the Socialists.
    (5) none of the above.

3. Canadian citizens who are _____ have the right to vote.
    (1) active in a political party
    (2) 18 years old and over
    (3) 21 years old and over
    (4) taxpayers
    (5) landowners

4. Which of the following is **not** an "access point"?
    (1) Voting
    (2) A parliamentary committee
    (3) The Cabinet
    (4) Informal meetings with high government officials
    (5) A caucus

5. The purpose of a royal commission is to
    (1) investigate government officials.
    (2) impeach high government officials.
    (3) hear public opinion on an important issue.
    (4) organize party campaigns.
    (5) canvass for parliamentary candidates.

6. How many political parties can there be in Canada?

    (1) One

    (2) Two

    (3) Three

    (4) Four

    (5) There is no limit.

7. How many political parties have dominated the government of Canada?

    (1) One

    (2) Two

    (3) Three

    (4) Many

    (5) None

8. The presence of political parties in Canada creates all of the following factors **except**

    (1) an egalitarian distribution of goods and services.

    (2) increased public participation in government.

    (3) control over the training and selection of candidates for public office.

    (4) the organization of campaigns.

    (5) political stability through the legitimizing of leaders.

Answer key

1. (1)

2. (5)

3. (2)

4. (1)

5. (3)

6. (5)

7. (2)

8. (1)

CANADIAN POLITICAL SYSTEM

Canada is defined by some as a constitutional monarchy and by others as a constitutional democracy. A **constitution** defines the limits of power for a democratic government. In 1867 Canadian leaders prepared the constitution, which was sent to the United Kingdom and approved by the British Parliament. Originally called the British North American Act of 1867, it was later renamed the Constitution Act. The document remained in the United Kingdom until the present government brought it within Canada's boundaries in 1982. The constitution had been amended 30 times before Canada took possession of it. The government of Canada can now amend the constitution without the approval of the British Parliament. The current document, known as the Constitution Act of 1982, provides Canada with a government that consists of three parts: Her Majesty the Queen, the Senate, and the House of Commons. The latter two branches form the Parliament of Canada.

Questions

The following questions refer to the preceding passage. Read each question and choose the correct answer.

1. The present name of the Canadian constitution is the

   (1) British North American Act of 1867.

   (2) Constitution Act of 1967.

   (3) British North American Act of 1982.

   (4) Constitution Act of 1982.

   (5) Constitution Act of 1867.

2. The three parts of Canada's government are

   (1) Congress, the Senate, and Her Majesty the Queen.

   (2) the Senate, the House of Commons, and the president.

   (3) Parliament, Her Majesty the Queen, and the president.

   (4) Her Majesty the Queen, the House of Commons, and the Senate.

   (5) none of the above.

3. A constitution defines the limits of power for

   (1) a democracy.

   (2) a nation-state.

   (3) an autocracy.

   (4) a monarchy.

   (5) both (1) and (2).

4. As of 1982, the government of Canada can amend its constitution by

   (1) an appeal to the Queen.

   (2) an appeal to the British Parliament.

   (3) an appeal to Congress.

   (4) sending it back to the United Kingdom.

   (5) none of the above.

Answers

1. (4)
2. (4)
3. (1)
4. (5)

ELECTIONS AND VOTING REGULATIONS

An independent body responsible to Parliament—called Elections Canada—is in charge of running federal elections. It does not make laws about elections, as this is done by Parliament. However, Elections Canada handles all details about printing ballots, choosing polling stations, appointing staff to run polling stations, counting ballots, and reporting results. The following extract comes from its Web site.

Who is entitled to vote?

You are entitled to vote in federal elections and referendums if you are a Canadian citizen, and will be 18 or older on polling day. See also section 3 of the Canada Elections Act.

If you are an elector (a person who is eligible to vote) and have been living away from Canada for less than five consecutive years since your last visit home, you are eligible to vote under The Special Voting Rules. You can register to vote at any time.

Incarcerated electors who are serving a prison sentence in a Canadian correctional institution have the right to vote in federal elections and referendums. For details, see Voting by Incarcerated Electors. You can also consult the October 31, 2002, press release on voting rights of incarcerated electors.

Can a person who is homeless vote?

Yes, an elector who is homeless or without a fixed address can vote, if he or she registers on the voters list during an election. To register, the elector must provide proof of identity and the address where he or she is staying. Proof of identity can be an official document bearing the elector's name and signature. For residence, the address of a local shelter is acceptable, if the elector slept there in the last 24 hours. Without such proof, a person who is homeless can register on election day by taking the prescribed oath as to identity and residence, as long as another voter who is registered in the same electoral district can vouch for that person.

Questions

The following questions refer to the preceding passage. Read each question and choose the best answer.

1. Which of the following is **not** a responsibility of Elections Canada?

   (1) Making laws about elections

   (2) Printing ballots

   (3) Choosing polling stations

   (4) Appointing staff to run polling stations

   (5) Counting ballots and reporting results

2. Which of the following Canadian citizens are not eligible to vote in federal elections?

   (1) A person who has lived outside Canada for four years

   (2) A person serving a sentence in a Canadian prison

   (3) A person without a fixed address

   (4) A homeless person

   (5) A 17-year-old person

Answers

1. (1)

2. (5)

CANADIAN POLITICAL SPECTRUM

When a beam of light shines through a glass prism, it splits into a spectrum (or range) of colours, from infrared to ultraviolet. Similarly, within Canada is a range of political viewpoints. This range is known as the political spectrum. Political parties that favour progressive income taxes (tax rates rise as income increases) and government involvement in the economy are called parties of the **left**. Parties that favour flat income taxes (every dollar earned is taxed at the same rate) and government staying out of the economy are called parties of the **right**. Between these two extremes are parties that favour some progression of income taxes and limited government involvement in the economy; these are called parties of the **centre**. Table 1 summarizes, in general terms, the range of views of the three main national political parties in Canada.

Questions

The following questions refer to the preceding passage and to Table 1. Read each question and choose the correct answer.

1. Which of the following people would be most likely to benefit from a flat income tax rate?

   (1) A poor person living on welfare

   (2) A professional person billing clients a total of $750 000 a year

Table 1. Canadian Political Spectrum

Party	Position on spectrum	Policy on taxation	Economy	Government intervention
New Democratic Party (NDP)	Left	Support progressive income taxes to make the rich pay a higher share than at present	Strong government presence through ownership of key utilities and vital national institutions	Government should be involved in the economy to ensure protection of national interest and fair distribution of economic resources among the people
Liberal	Centre	Support limited progressivity of income taxes, but taxes should not be so high as to discourage the rich from working hard	Privately owned businesses are more efficient and should be encouraged, but there may be a need for limited government ownership of key utilities	Government should stay out of trying to regulate the economy, except under specific circumstances that require it
Conservative	Right	Income taxes should be flat; people are discouraged from working hard if their tax burden rises as a result	Privately owned businesses are more efficient; existing government-owned utilities and businesses should be privatized	The private sector should be left alone, and government should confine itself to issues of national security and foreign policy

(3)   A person employed full-time at the minimum wage rate

(4)   A university student employed part-time for 20 hours a week

(5)   A full-time elementary school teacher at the top of the pay scale

2.   Which party is likely to be the strongest supporter of ending government ownership of hydro companies?

(1)   Conservatives

(2)   All parties

(3)   New Democratic Party

(4)   None of the parties

(5)   Liberals

3.   Which party is most likely to be in favor of government support for bankrupt companies like Air Canada?

(1)   Conservatives

(2)   All parties within the spectrum

(3)   New Democratic Party

(4)   None of the parties within the spectrum

(5)   Liberals

Answers

1.   (2)

2.   (1)

3.   (3)

"UNITE THE RIGHT" CAMPAIGN, 2000–2004

Synergy: "Increased effectiveness, achievement, etc., produced by combined action, co-operation, etc." [from Katherine Barber, ed., *The Canadian Oxford Dictionary* (Toronto, ON: Oxford University Press Canada, 1998), 1471].

After the election of the third consecutive majority Liberal government in 2000, some members of the Canadian Alliance and Progressive Conservative parties decided they had to work to unite their two parties. If the two parties remained separate, they reasoned, they would split the votes of conservatives (the right) and continue to lose to the Liberals. Some members of both parties were opposed to the idea, but in 2003 both parties finally agreed to unite in a party called the Conservative Party of Canada. They planned to run their first campaign as a single party in the federal election of 2004.

Some people believed that the larger Canadian Alliance would dominate the new party and that the Progressive Conservatives would gradually get squeezed out. Figure 1 is a cartoon that appeared in the *Globe and Mail*, which calls itself "Canada's national newspaper."

Figure 1.
Reprinted with permission from the Globe and Mail.

Question

The following questions refer to Figure 1. Read the question and choose the correct answer.

1. What is the cartoonist saying about the union of the Progressive Conservatives and the Canadian Alliance?

    (1) The Progressive Conservatives have added significant strength to the Canadian Alliance.

    (2) The Progressive Conservatives will be able to move the Canadian Alliance in a new direction.

    (3) The Progressive Conservatives are insignificant as a force in the new united party.

    (4) The Progressive Conservatives and the Canadian Alliance are moving toward the political centre.

    (5) The Progressive Conservatives and the Canadian Alliance are going to win the next federal election.

Answer

1. (3)

NATIONAL EXECUTIVE BRANCH

The executive branch is headed by Her Majesty the Queen. She is represented in Canada by the governor-general, who in turn is advised by the prime minister and the Cabinet. The governor-general's role in a constitutional monarchy is to represent the monarch as head of state. The governor-general ensures that there is always a prime minister and a responsible Cabinet in office. The Cabinet advises but does not control the governor-general. The governor-general also serves as a mediator between political party leaders on issues of national concern. In exceptional circumstances the governor-general has exercised reserve power and has refused to act as the Cabinet would have preferred. Generally, the governor-general displays benevolence within and sometimes outside Canada's borders. The head of state should also provide moral and social leadership for the good of national living conditions.

The Cabinet is the centre of government in Canada and consists of (1) the prime minister, normally the leader of the ruling party with extraordinary powers; (2) other ministers who are political heads of the government's bureaucratic departments; and (3) ministers without portfolio, such as government party senators, the government's leader in the Senate, and other members of Parliament needed to fill regional or other quotas to balance the Cabinet. The Cabinet is the committee that links the governor-general (the head of state) with the Parliament (the people's representatives). For all practical purposes, the Cabinet is the real executive. R. MacGregor Dawson, who was one of Canada's most famous early political scientists, describes the Cabinet's responsibilities as the following: (1) formulating and performing all executive policies, (2) administering all government departments, (3) providing guidance to the legislative programs of the government, and (4) managing nearly all the government's finances. Even though the Cabinet serves the purposes of the governor-general, in practice the Cabinet recommends actions that the governor-general must follow in most cases. By serving the Parliament, the Cabinet also acts as the leader and guide to legislative reforms. This glue that holds the core of government together is not mentioned in the Constitution Act of 1867 or in the Constitution Act of 1982; however, historical precedent, known as convention, has enshrined the purpose and practical usefulness of the Cabinet.

The public service provides consistent public policy during transition periods of the government, such as when a new ruling party takes power. The public service helps the government to implement changes according to the new laws enacted by Parliament. As an access point for its citizens, the public service provides details from research, citizens, pressure groups, and historical data, all of which helps to formulate new legislation and changes in society. The deputy minister of a department is a senior public servant who is directly responsible to the department cabinet minister. In turn, the cabinet minister is accountable to the Cabinet and the House of Commons. This direct accountability of bureaucracy to the Cabinet and the Cabinet to its citizens' representatives comprises a system that is both responsible and representative.

Questions

The following questions refer to the preceding passage. Read each question and choose the correct answer.

1. The governor-general's role is to

    (1) ensure that there is a prime minister and a responsible Cabinet in office.

    (2) act as a mediator between political party leaders on issues of national concern.

    (3) make gestures of goodwill within and sometimes outside Canada.

    (4) all of the above.

    (5) none of the above.

2. Which of the following is **not** a member of the Cabinet?

    (1) Ministers of government departments

    (2) Prime minister

    (3) Government party members of Parliament

    (4) Government party senators

    (5) None of the above

3. The political hierarchy of Canada from top to bottom is

    (1) Her Majesty the Queen, the Cabinet, the governor-general, and the prime minister.

    (2) Her Majesty the Queen, the prime minister, the governor-general, and the Cabinet.

    (3) Her Majesty the Queen, the governor-general, the prime minister, and the Cabinet.

    (4) the Cabinet, Her Majesty the Queen, the governor-general, and the prime minister.

    (5) none of the above.

Answers

1. (4)

2. (3)

3. (3)

NATIONAL LEGISLATIVE BRANCH

The legislative branch consists of the Senate and the House of Commons, known collectively as the Canadian Parliament. The House of Commons is the popularly elected lower house, often considered an uncontrolled arena of liberalism. The Senate is the upper house and is regarded as a place of "sober second thought." This **bicameral** ("two-house") legislature exists in approximately 50 countries around the world.

The senators were originally appointed for life, but now they must retire at the age of 75 years old. They represent the four major regions of Canada, with 24 from each area: the Maritime Provinces, the Western Provinces, Quebec, and Ontario. Eight more come from other areas: six from Newfoundland, one from the Yukon Territory, and one from the Northwest Territories. When vacancies become available, a new senator is appointed by the prime minister.

The Senate considers legislation that has been prepared by parliamentary committees and the public service and has been approved by the Cabinet and the House of Commons. The Senate can approve, reject, or amend the bills it receives. If the bill is approved by both houses, it is sent to the governor-general, who will sign it in the presence of both houses. Once the governor-general signs the bill, it has "royal assent" and becomes law. The bill then changes to an act; for example Bill 99 would become Act 99.

The Senate may initiate bills, as private members of Parliament can, with some restrictions. If the majority of the House of Commons rejects a government bill, the prime minister usually gives his resignation to the governor-general. This is a Canadian conception of responsible government. The governor-general may then dissolve the House of Commons and order a federal election. An exception to this precedent occurred in 1926, when Lord Byng refused to dissolve the nine-month-old House comprising an opposition with 116 members and the government with 101 members.

The House of Commons is occupied by members of Parliament (MPs) elected by people of various electoral ridings scattered throughout Canada. The MPs are voted in for a maximum of five years. The party with the largest number of MPs elected to the House becomes the cornerstone of the government, and its leader, the prime minister, appoints the Cabinet from the party's members of Parliament. The leader of the opposition is the leader of the political party with the second-largest number of members in the House of Commons. By law, the House of Commons must open at least once a year for business matters. At that time, bills are submitted and every member has an opportunity to address the current issues. Votes are then taken to pass or reject any proposed bills.

Questions

The following questions refer to the preceding passage. Read each question and choose the correct answer.

1. The national legislative branch of Canada is

    (1) a single-house legislature.

    (2) a bicameral legislature.

    (3) known collectively as Congress.

    (4) popularly elected.

    (5) none of the above.

2. Each of the following describes a characteristic of senators **except**

    (1) they are appointed by Her Majesty the Queen.

    (2) they must resign at the age of 75.

    (3) they may initiate bills.

    (4) they may reject or amend bills.

    (5) none of the above.

3. Which of the following statements is **false**?

    (1) The prime minister may dissolve the Parliament.

    (2) When a bill receives royal assent from the governor-general's signature, it becomes an act.

    (3) The prime minister appoints the senators in the event of a vacancy.

    (4) When a government bill is rejected by the House of Commons, the prime minister usually submits his resignation to the governor-general.

    (5) None of the above

4. Which of the following statements is **true**?

    (1) A bill becomes an act after being signed by Her Majesty the Queen in the presence of both houses.

    (2) The House of Commons is required to be open for business only once a year.

    (3) Members of Parliament must retire at the age of 75.

    (4) The Yukon Territory has only six senators.

    (5) The governor-general is the leader of the party in power.

Answers

1. (2)

2. (1)

3. (1)

4. (2)

NATIONAL JUDICIAL BRANCH

There are three kinds of law in Canada. The first is **statutory law**, the criminal code. The second is **common law**, which is primarily unwritten social norms. The third is **civil law**, a code law that was imported by the French and applies only to the Province of Quebec.

The Supreme Court of Canada is the highest court in the land, and its decisions are binding on the lower courts. The role of the Supreme Court is to ensure a balance between the laws and policies of government and the rights of the various sectors of society. These rights are outlined in the Charter of Rights and Freedoms, which is part of the Constitution Act of 1982. This structure is similar to the United States' Bill of Rights in the Constitution. The Supreme Court of Canada can overrule acts and executive powers it deems unconstitutional.

Courts in Canada are instituted to protect the rights of its citizens. A common example of the Canadian court system can be found in the Province of Saskatchewan. At the top is the Supreme Court of Canada, the federal court. Next is the Exchequer Court of Canada; it hears cases against the Crown. The Court of Appeal is a provincial court composed of federally appointed judges; it deals with criminal and civil cases. The Court of the Queen's Bench, which also has federally appointed judges and deals with criminal and civil cases, hears some appeals as well. The District Court for Saskatchewan has federally appointed judges and hears appeals from minor provincial courts; it also handles cases involving less than $5000 worth of claims. The final level of the judicial branch is composed of the minor courts, which handle four different categories of cases:

1. The Surrogate Court for Saskatchewan oversees wills, estates, and the estates of the deceased.

2. Provincial magistrates deal with lower appeals.

3. Justices of the peace deal with charges under municipal bylaws and some provincial or federal laws.

4. The rest of the minor courts handle family and juvenile law and other special cases.

Minor court judges are appointed by the queen's representative, with the lieutenant governor in counsel. This hierarchy of courts is similar in each Canadian province.

Questions

The following questions refer to the preceding passage. Read each question and choose the correct answer.

1. Which of the following statements about Canadian law is **false**?

   (1) Statutory law is the criminal code for all of Canada.

   (2) Common law represents unwritten social norms.

   (3) Civil law is a code law that originates from France and applies only in the Province of Saskatchewan.

   (4) There are only three main types of law in Canada.

   (5) None of the above

2. The Supreme Court of Canada makes decisions based on which of the following?

   (1) Charter of Rights and Freedoms

   (2) Bill of Rights

   (3) Charter of Rights and Freedoms and Constitution Act of 1982

   (4) Bill of Rights and British North American Act of 1867

   (5) Constitution Act of 1867

3. Which provincial court hears appeals against the Crown?

   (1) Court of Appeal

   (2) Court of the Queen's Bench

   (3) District Court

   (4) Supreme Court of Canada

   (5) Exchequer Court of Canada

Answers

1. (3)

2. (3)

3. (5)

GED Social Studies

Geography

GEOGRAPHY

GEOGRAPHY PRINCIPLES AND CONCEPTS

The earth is a sphere; that is, its shape resembles that of a ball. Geographers have drawn imaginary lines, known as lines of latitude and longitude, on the earth to pinpoint locations. Lines of latitude run parallel to each other from the equator, the east–west circumference of the earth. Moving away from the equator, latitude numbers increase to a maximum of 90° N or 90° S. Lines of longitude run north–south through the North and South poles. The line through Greenwich, England (known as the Greenwich or prime meridian) is 0°, and longitude numbers increase moving east or west of that line to a maximum of 180° E or 180° W. Places furthest away from the equator have the highest latitude numbers, while places furthest away from the Greenwich meridian have the highest longitude numbers. Latitude is stated first and longitude second.

Geographers draw maps to represent particular features on the earth. These maps are drawn to scale, so that 1 cm on the map represents a particular distance on the earth. On a scale of 1 cm to 80 000 000 cm (or 1:80 000 000), almost the entire earth could be represented on a sheet of foolscap paper. As more detail is required, scale is altered to include less distance in the standard 1-cm space. The same sheet of foolscap paper could show all of Canada on a scale of 1:17 000 000 (1 cm to 170 km) or metropolitan Toronto on a scale of 1:250 000 (1 cm to 2.5 km).

Physical geographers draw maps to show geology (rock types), topography (hills and valleys), climate, soil types, vegetation, and resources. Human geographers draw maps to population patterns, ethnic distribution, and language(s) spoken in a particular region.

Canada can be divided into regions based on their various features. For example, Vancouver's weather is wet and mild, which puts it clearly in a different climate region from that of Winnipeg, where it is dry and the temperatures extreme. Also, the grey-brown Podzol soils of southern Ontario place that area in a different soil region from the black Chernozem soils of southern Manitoba.

Regional variations are also evident in Canada's complex economy. Agriculture is very important to most southern regions. In Saskatchewan, for example, wheat farming predominates. In the Okanagan Valley of British Columbia, the Niagara Peninsula of Ontario, and the Annapolis Valley of Nova Scotia, fruit farming is an important activity. Canada also has a large mining sector offering coal from Nova Scotia and Alberta, copper from Ontario and British Columbia, and iron ore from Quebec. Forestry is extensive in Ontario and even more so in British Columbia, where it constitutes the largest part of the economy of any province. Fishing is an important employer and generator of income in the Atlantic and Pacific regions. Oil and gas production is important in Alberta, Saskatchewan, the Northwest Territories, and off the coast of Newfoundland.

To move products from one region to another or for export, an extensive transportation system has developed. Rail lines take goods to cities like Halifax and Vancouver, where they can easily be transferred to oceangoing ships. Pipelines carry oil and gas throughout Canada and directly into the United States. Large trucks carry finished goods by road to delivery points, while rail, bus, and airline routes carry people to distant destinations.

Questions

Questions 1 and 2 refer to Figure 1. Read each question and choose the correct answer.

1. The location of Cairo would be correctly stated as

    (1) 25° N, 30° W.

    (2) 10° N, 15° E.

    (3) 25° S, 25° W.

    (4) 30° N, 30° E.

    (5) 15° N, 15° E.

2. Another way of stating the scale of the map in Figure 1 is

    (1) 1 cm to 1 km.

    (2) 1 cm to 10 km.

    (3) 1 cm to 100 km.

    (4) 1 cm to 1000 km.

    (5) 1 cm to 10 000 km.

Questions 3–5 refer to Table 1. Read each question and then choose the correct answer.

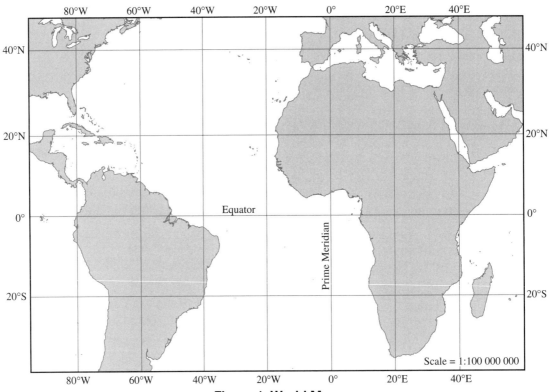

Figure 1. World Map

Table 1. Locations of Major Canadian Cities

City	Latitude	Longitude
Victoria	48°26' N	123°20' W
Montreal	45°32' N	73°36' W
Halifax	44°40' N	63°41' W
Winnipeg	49°53' N	97°10' W
St. John's	47°34' N	52°43' W

3. Which of these cities is situated closest to the North Pole?

   (1) Victoria

   (2) Montreal

   (3) Halifax

   (4) Winnipeg

   (5) St. John's

4. Which of these cities would experience sunset the earliest?

   (1) Victoria

   (2) Montreal

   (3) Halifax

   (4) Winnipeg

   (5) St. John's

5. Which of these cities is farthest from the prime meridian?

   (1) Victoria

   (2) Montreal

   (3) Halifax

   (4) Winnipeg

   (5) St. John's

Questions 6 and 7 refer to Figure 2 and the text that follows.

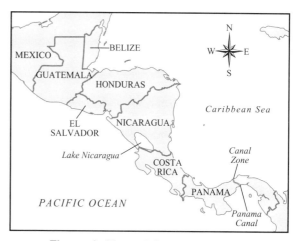

Figure 2. Map of Central America

Culturally, Central America is part of Latin America, which refers to the colonial influence of the Spanish "Latin" rulers from the 1500s until almost the 20th century in some areas. Geographically, Central America is part of North America. Historically, it was the site of the great empire of the Maya. As a result of this variety, the people of Central America have a rich mixture of ethnic and cultural heritage. Today Central American nations strive to keep their national independence and to raise their standard of living.

6. Central America includes all **except**

   (1) Colombia.

   (2) Nicaragua.

   (3) Panama.

   (4) Costa Rica.

   (5) Guatemala.

7. Which is **not** a characteristic of Central America?

    (1) It is part of North America.

    (2) It has access to two oceans.

    (3) Its heritage is modeled solely on the Spanish influence.

    (4) It has strategic importance as a major trade artery.

    (5) It contains nations that need economic assistance.

Answers

1. (4)

2. (4)

3. (4)

4. (5)

5. (1)

6. (1)

7. (3)

CANADIAN REGIONS

Canada may be divided into several economic regions. An **economic region** is an area in which a single type, or very small number of different types, of commercial activity predominate.

In the Prairie Provinces (Alberta, Saskatchewan, and Manitoba), wheat and cattle farming are important to the economy. Because British Columbia is a mountainous province, agriculture is not practical in most areas. Vast timber forests grow there, however, and forestry dominates the economy, providing much employment and wealth. Canada's largest concentration of manufacturing plants is situated in southern Ontario. Together with southern Quebec, this region is frequently referred to as the Industrial Heartland.

In the Maritime Provinces (Newfoundland, Nova Scotia, New Brunswick, and Prince Edward Island), fishing, forestry, and agriculture are a large part of the economy. The great distances between this Atlantic region and the heaviest concentration of population (in southern Ontario) make it an unattractive location for industrial plants. As a result, manufacturing industries have been reluctant to locate there.

Regions may be defined not only by economic activity but also by geography. A good example of this would be the North. It may be further divided into the Near North and the Far North. See Figure 3.

The Near North is home to boreal forests, which are composed almost entirely of coniferous trees like fir and spruce. Further north, boreal forests become more prevalent because leaf-bearing trees do not grow abundantly in the region's harsh climate. In the Far North the climate becomes progressively more extreme. North of $66 \frac{1}{2}°$ N, the sun shines 24 hours a day at the height of summer, but it does not rise above the horizon in midwinter. Forests exist only at the southern edge of the Far North. In its northern portions, where there is any vegetation at all, it is confined to short grasses, mosses, and lichens.

Much of Canada's economic wealth has been generated through the consumption of its resources. Minerals like coal, gas, oil, iron, and nickel have been exported in huge quantities, bringing in much revenue from abroad. These resources, however, are not renewable; that is, they cannot be replaced, except in a time scale of millions of years. Concern is therefore rising that Canada's economic growth is not sustainable. Once the nation's resources are used up, the argument runs, its economic growth will inevitably slow. More emphasis is now being placed on developing renewable resources to ensure sustainable growth.

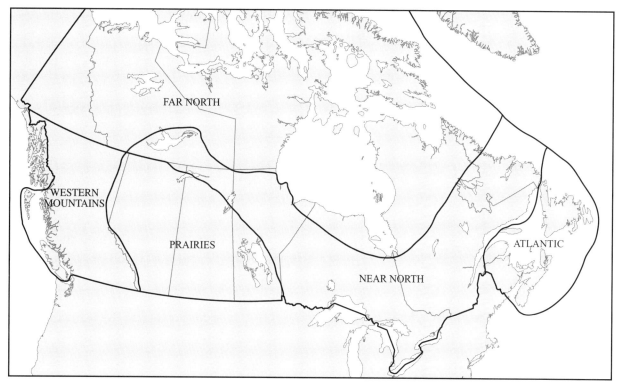

Figure 3. Canadian Regions

Questions

The following questions refer to the preceding passage. Read each question and choose the correct answer.

1. Which of the following would **not** be considered an economic region?

    (1) Southern Ontario and southern Quebec

    (2) Prairie Provinces

    (3) Alberta and British Columbia

    (4) Atlantic Canada

    (5) Yukon Territory

2. Which of the following would **not** be a reason that forestry predominates as an economic activity in British Columbia?

    (1) The presence of large timber tracts

    (2) The existence of efficient ocean terminals in Vancouver for exporting to the Pacific Rim

    (3) Heavy-duty rail links to connect to large markets in the United States

    (4) A provincial corporate tax system that favours resource companies

    (5) The imposition by the United States of tariffs on imported lumber

3. Which of the following items is **most** likely to be produced in the Industrial Heartland?

   (1) Wheat

   (2) Lumber

   (3) Fruit

   (4) Tractors

   (5) Fish

4. Which of the following is an example of a coniferous tree?

   (1) Pine

   (2) Oak

   (3) Beech

   (4) Maple

   (5) Hickory

5. Which of the following would be considered a renewable resource?

   (1) Oil

   (2) Coal

   (3) Gas

   (4) Nuclear power

   (5) Solar power

6. Although Dawson City, Yukon Territory, is located at latitude 64° N, daily high temperatures in July frequently reach 25°C. Which of the following factors **most** likely contributes to this?

   (1) The sun is low in the sky.

   (2) Westerly winds blow in from the Pacific Ocean.

   (3) The town is situated 500 metres above sea level.

   (4) The sun shines almost 24 hours a day.

   (5) There are many cloudy days.

Questions 7 and 8 refer to the climate graphs depicted in Figure 4. Read each question and choose the correct answer.

7. What does the curved graph line represent?

   (1) Precipitation

   (2) Hours of sunlight

   (3) Temperature

   (4) Wind strength

   (5) Barometric pressure

8. What does the stepped graph line represent?

   (1) Precipitation

   (2) Hours of sunlight

   (3) Temperature

   (4) Wind strength

   (5) Barometric pressure

Answers

1. (3)

2. (5)

3. (4)

4. (1)

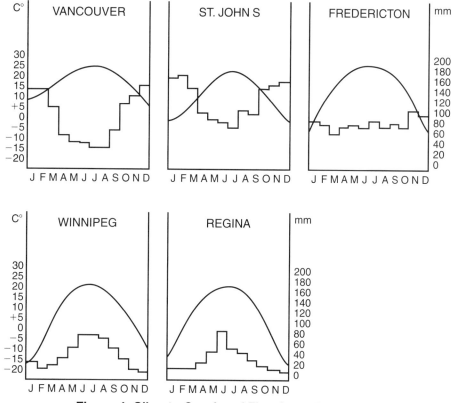

**Figure 4. Climate Graphs of Five Canadian Cities,
Showing Temperatue (left scale) and Precipitation (right scale)**

5. (5)

6. (4)

7. (3)

8. (1)

POPULATION GROWTH

Four factors contribute to the growth or reduction of a nation's population. Births and immigration (people coming into the nation) raise the population, while deaths and emigration (people leaving the nation) reduce it. In general, the populations of developed countries are rising slowly. In many of these countries, the death rate is higher than the birth rate, which would lead to population decline in the long run. But immigration greatly exceeds emigration, and the net effect of all this is that populations are rising. In most developing nations, birth rates exceed death rates, and this factor alone results in steadily rising populations. There are, of course, exceptions to all these generalizations. In Russia—a developed country—the population is in slow but steady decline. And many developing nations in Africa have been so significantly effected by the epidemic of HIV/AIDS that population levels in them are actually falling.

Table 2. Population Growth and Reduction Factors in Canada, 2000–2001

2000 population	Births	Immigrants	Deaths	Emigrants
30 792 567	329 791	252 088	227 076	65 483

Question

The following question refers to Table 2. Read the question and choose the correct answer.

1. What was Canada's population in 2001?

    (1) 30 503 247

    (2) 31 031 863

    (3) 30 552 371

    (4) 31 081 887

    (5) 31 068 576

Answer

1. (4)

POPULATION PYRAMIDS

Geographers use so-called population pyramids to illustrate the age distribution of individual countries. As shown in Figure 5, each age band, represented by a horizontal bar, is a percentage of the total, with males on the left and females on the right.

Questions

The following questions refer to Figure 5. Read each question and choose the correct answer.

1. Which of the following pieces of information may **not** be derived from the population pyramid?

    (1) The total percentage of males and females in the population

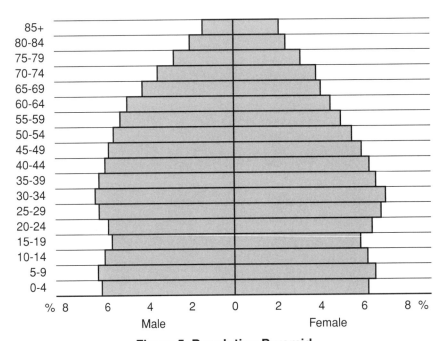

Figure 5. Population Pyramid

(2) The percentage of the total that males and females in the 25–29 age group represent

(3) The comparative size of the population in the 5–9 and 60–64 age groups

(4) The increase or decrease in the population

(5) The percentage of the population 85 years and older

2. What conclusion may be correctly drawn from the population pyramid?

(1) The birth rate has declined over the past 10 years.

(2) The death rate has increased over the past 10 years.

(3) The birth rate has increased over the past 10 years.

(4) The death rate has declined over the past 10 years.

(5) The birth and death rates have been steady over the past 10 years.

Answers

1. (4)

2. (1)

PRIMARY, SECONDARY, AND TERTIARY SECTORS AND GROSS DOMESTIC PRODUCT

A nation's gross domestic product (GDP) is the total of all the goods and services it produces in a year. The GDP can be generated from three sectors: the primary sector comprises agricultural and other resource-based industries; the secondary sector comprises manufacturing; and the tertiary sector comprises the sales and service industries. Table 3 illustrates some significant differences. Wealth generation tends to be least in the primary sector and most in the tertiary sector. All the countries shown are real.

Questions

The following questions refer to Table 3. Read each question and choose the correct answer.

1. Which country is **most** likely to be a developed, industrial nation?

(1) Country A

(2) Country B

(3) Country C

(4) Country D

(5) Country E

Table 3. Percentage Employed in Various Sectors, 2000

Country	Primary* (%)	Secondary† (%)	Tertiary‡ (%)
A	85	5	10
B	11	45	44
C	6	35	59
D	47	18	35
E	71	14	15

*Agriculture and other resource-based industries
†Manufacturing
‡Sales and service industries

2. Which country is likely to have the lowest standard of living?

    (1) Country A

    (2) Country B

    (3) Country C

    (4) Country D

    (5) Country E

Answers

1. (3)

2. (1)

FIRST LANGUAGES

English and French are the official languages of Canada. This means that the federal government and the federal courts operate in these two languages. Canadians have the right to communicate with their member of Parliament in either official language, and to be tried in a federal court in a similar manner. Provincial legislation on language is widely varied. New Brunswick is the only province that is officially bilingual. Quebec is officially unilingual in French, and the other provinces are officially unilingual in English. Even in the unilingual provinces, however, many services are offered in both official languages. (Education is a good example.) But in those provinces, there are clear limits set to the amount of bilingual services available.

Just because English and French are official languages does not mean that they are considered more worthy than other languages. It's just that governments have a limit to the number of services that they can offer. Many Canadians speak a first language at home that is neither English nor French. (A **first language**, sometimes called a mother tongue, is defined as the first language a person learned and still understands.) But they are expected to be functional in one of the official languages if they want to participate fully in Canadian society. Many school districts offer heritage language programs, which teach the language and culture of specific linguistic and cultural groups. But these are normally taught outside the school day, and the regular program is taught in one of the official languages.

Table 4. Percentage of Population by First Language in Selected Canadian Provinces and Territories, 2001

Province/ territory	English	French	Other
New Brunswick	65.2	33.1	1.7
Nunavut	26.4	1.5	72.1
Ontario	71.6	4.4	24.0
Saskatchewan	85.8	1.9	12.3
Manitoba	75.8	4.1	20.1

Questions

The following questions refer to Table 4. Read each question and choose the correct answer.

1. In which province or territory did the smallest percentage of people have a language other than English or French as their first language?

    (1) New Brunswick

    (2) Nunavut

    (3) Ontario

    (4) Saskatchewan

    (5) Manitoba

2. Which of the following conclusions may be correctly drawn from the information in Table 4?

   (1) English is growing in popularity as a first language in the provinces and territories listed.

   (2) In every province or territory listed, most people speak English as their first language.

   (3) In Nunavut (the Northwest Territories) most people speak a first language other than English or French.

   (4) A greater proportion of people speak French as a first language in Saskatchewan than in Manitoba.

   (5) A smaller proportion of people speak French as a first language in Ontario than in Manitoba.

Answers

1. (1)

2. (3)

CULTURAL REGIONS OF THE WORLD

As shown in Figure 6, the world can be divided into many cultural regions, such as the Anglo-American, European, and Sino-Japanese regions. These regions differ significantly from each other when their physical environments, economic development, and cultural compositions are studied.

Physically, North America consists of a wide variety of features. From the tundra of Alaska to the prairies of Alberta and Saskatchewan to the swampland of the Mississippi delta, enormous climatic and geological differences can be observed. The Middle East, by contrast, appears to be more uniform in its physical environment. Being confined to the lower latitudes, its climate is uniformly hot and rainfall generally low. Accordingly, irrigation of the land is necessary for successful commercial farming. The Pacific Rim contains countries such as Japan, Taiwan, Singapore, Australia, and New Zealand. Here large physical differences are again observable, from the

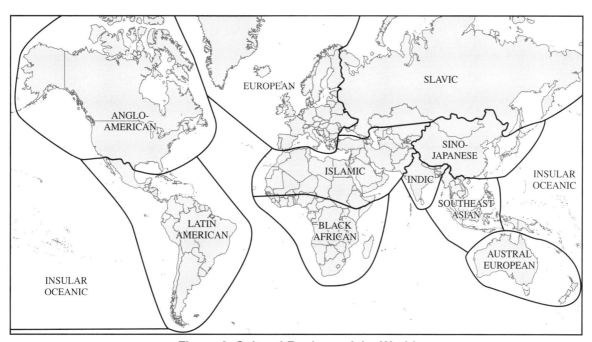

Figure 6. Cultural Regions of the World

rocky islands of Japan and New Zealand to the desertlike Nullarbor Plain of central Australia.

Great variations also exist among the cultural regions of the world in terms of their economic development. Industrial methods of production have dominated for more than a century in western Europe and North America, producing high living standards for their inhabitants. Since the 1950s Japan has undergone a change from traditional to modern industrial methods. Within the last quarter century countries in the Pacific Rim—like South Korea, Singapore, and Taiwan—have experienced similar changes. But other regions have not experienced modernization. Countries like Tanzania and Mozambique, in sub-Saharan Africa, still lack an industrial economy. Subsistence farming and small-scale factories still dominate the economies there, and living standards tend to be lower.

The total value of all the goods and services produced in a year in an individual country is called the gross domestic product (GDP). Generally, countries with greater levels of industrial production have higher levels of GDP for each member of the population (GDP per capita), while less industrialized countries have lower levels. For example, in 2005 the GDP per capita (in U.S. dollars) in Canada was just over $32 800; the GDP in most western European countries was in the $25 000–$30 000 range; Japan at $30 000 and South Korea at $19 400 had closed or were closing the gap; and nonindustrial countries like Tanzania ($610) and Sudan ($2 100) had much lower living standards.

The world's regions also differ culturally. While Christianity and Judaism have predominated in western Europe and North and South America, Islam has been very influential in North Africa and the Middle East. Hinduism dominates the religious life of India, and Buddhism is the leading religion in many other parts of Asia. Religious thought has had an influence on the basic values of these regions. Christianity and Judaism appear to have adopted a more flexible interpretation of male and female roles than, for example, has Islam. Accordingly, women in western countries have more choices available to them than do their counterparts in strict Muslim countries.

In the latter half of the 20th century, the world's cultural regions recognized that they could not remain entirely separate from one another. If we are to solve global problems, such as global warming or uncontrolled population growth, the regions must cooperate.

Questions

The following questions refer to the preceding passage. Read each question and choose the correct answer.

1. Which of the following conclusions about the world's regions can be correctly drawn from the passage?

   (1) Physical and cultural regions are not always identical.

   (2) The world's cultural regions are at similar levels of economic development.

   (3) Industrial methods of production were adopted at approximately the same time in the world's various regions.

   (4) The Sino-Japanese cultural region was one of the first to industrialize.

   (5) Subsistence farming has largely disappeared in the sub-Saharan or black African region.

Question 2 is based on Figure 6.

2. Which of the following conclusions can be reached from studying the map?

    (1) All of Asia forms one culture realm.

    (2) Cultural regions in Africa tend to closely follow political boundaries.

    (3) People of the North American continent share a common cultural heritage.

    (4) Religion and ethnic origin separates African cultural regions.

    (5) None of the above

3. Why is irrigation of the land necessary for commercial farming in the Middle East?

    (1) There are many mountains.

    (2) The land consists of rocky islands.

    (3) The climate is hot and rainfall low.

    (4) The Nullarbor Plain is like a desert.

    (5) The land consists of tundra.

4. When one compares the physical regions of the world, which of the following can one observe to be correct?

    (1) They are basically similar.

    (2) All countries in the Pacific Rim are rocky islands.

    (3) Some regions are uniform in their features, while other regions are diverse.

    (4) North America is situated in the middle latitudes.

    (5) The Middle East is a diverse region.

5. Which of the following statements about GDP per capita and levels of industrialization is true?

    (1) Countries with high levels of industry have low levels of GDP per capita.

    (2) Countries with low levels of industry have high levels of GDP per capita.

    (3) There is no link between levels of GDP per capita and levels of industry.

    (4) Countries with high levels of industry have high levels of GDP per capita.

    (5) High levels of GDP per capita cause high levels of industry.

Answers

1. (1)

2. (4)

3. (3)

4. (3)

5. (4)

USING THE WORLD'S RESOURCES

Until recently, many people believed that the world's population would rapidly outstrip food supplies and that hunger and malnutrition would greatly increase. Despite a twofold increase in population since 1950, the food supply on this planet has nearly tripled. Unfortunately, most of that increase is in the hands, or rather the mouths, of the rich nations, while a billion people in Latin America, Africa, and Asia still go hungry.

Many of the world's richest nations are those possessing large amounts of natural resources. The wealth of the Middle East, for example, comes largely from the huge deposits of oil found there. South Africa has vast quantities of gold, chromium, and diamonds. Canada possesses oil, iron, nickel, and many other valuable resources. But mere possession of natural resources is insufficient to ensure wealth for a nation's inhabitants. Many other conditions need to be in place before riches can be realized, including capital to develop mining or refining facilities, an available supply of skilled and unskilled labour to develop and staff such operations, a good education system to provide basic skills to prospective employees, and transportation links to get the resource to its final destination speedily and cheaply.

As nations become more developed, an increasing proportion of its people tend to live in urban centres. This trend has become more pronounced in the period since the end of World War II. In 1965, 67 per cent of Japan's population lived in urban centres, a figure that had risen to 78 per cent by 1985. In South Korea this trend was even more pronounced, as the urban population rose from 32 per cent to 65 per cent in the same period. Urban populations provide pools of labour to work in large-scale industrial operations. Universities and colleges of technology to train people can be established more effectively in urban areas than in rural areas. The link between industrialization and urbanization is strong.

In the early state of an industrializing nation, growth is likely to be valued above all else. Nations try to expand their employment and output figures by building larger plants.

Worker income tends to rise at this stage, creating a general sense of confidence. At an intermediate stage, however, most industrializing nations realize that they are achieving a good deal of their growth at the expense of the environment. Land, air, water, and noise pollution have a tendency to increase, causing health and stress problems among the population. At a later stage governments usually place limitations on the amounts of pollution plants may emit. Reducing pollution output to tolerable levels is enormously expensive, and profits from industry may well decline while this problem is addressed. But the 1990s have seen the development of a final stage marked by a growing realization that while development is desirable, only sustainable development should be encouraged. This means that development is only desirable if it avoids impossible strains on the world's resources or environment.

Another feature of the modern world is the growth of international trade. Organizations such as the European Community (EC) have grown in importance in international trade. Twelve countries, with a combined population of 340 000 000, belong to the EC. Trade among EC countries proceeds without tariffs and quotas. Automobiles built in Spain are sold free of duties in Britain and Italy. French textiles are sold without special import taxes in Germany. In August 1992 the governments of the United States, Canada, and Mexico signed an agreement to create a North American Free Trade Association (NAFTA). Many economists believe that such international trade organizations, in which many countries will form a large trading bloc, will become increasingly common in the future.

Questions

The following questions refer to the preceding passage. Read each question and choose the correct answer.

1. Apart from the mere possession of natural resources, which of the following is a requirement to ensure wealth for a nation's inhabitants?

    (1) Capital to develop mining or refining

    (2) Availability of skilled and unskilled labour

    (3) A good education system to train prospective employees

    (4) Transportation links to get the resource to its final destination

    (5) All the above

2. Which of the following statements is **not** a reason or example of why the link between industrialization and urbanization is strong?

    (1) Between 1965 and 1985 Japan's urban population rose from 67 per cent to 78 per cent of its total population.

    (2) Urban populations can provide large pools of labour to work in industrial plants.

    (3) South Korea's urban population rose from 32 per cent to 65 per cent of its total population between 1965 and 1985.

    (4) Universities and colleges to train people in the skills needed by industries can be established more effectively in urban centers than in rural areas.

    (5) Urban populations can place restrictions on industries more effectively than rural populations can.

3. In which stage of a nation's industrialization process is growth likely to be valued above all else?

    (1) When industrialization is talked about but not actually begun

    (2) During the early stage, as nations expand their employment and output

    (3) At an intermediate stage, when the nation realizes that growth is being achieved at the expense of the environment

    (4) At a later stage, when limits are put on the amount of pollution a plant may emit

    (5) In the final stage, when nations realize that only sustainable development is desirable

4. Which of the following do many economists believe is likely to become increasingly common in the future as far as international trade is concerned?

    (1) A reduction in international trade around the world

    (2) Increases in tariffs (import duties) on goods brought in from another country

    (3) Each country will be responsible for making as many of the products as it needs

    (4) The growth of international trading organizations in which many countries will form a large trading bloc

    (5) Countries like Canada, the United States, and Mexico going their own way in international trade matters

Questions 5 and 6 refer to the preceding passage and to Figures 7 and 8. Read each question and choose the correct answer.

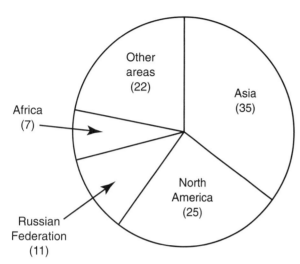

Figure 7. Percentage of World Energy Production, Selected Areas, 2000

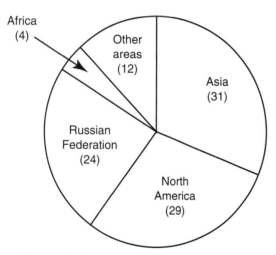

Figure 8. Percentage of World Energy Consumption, Selected Areas, 2000

5. Which area had the greatest energy deficit (that is, consumed more than it produced)?

   (1) Asia

   (2) North America

   (3) Russian Federation

   (4) Africa

   (5) Other areas

6. Which of the following statements may **not** be correctly inferred from Figures 7 and 8?

   (1) Asia consumed more than it produced.

   (2) Africa was the smallest consumer.

   (3) Other areas had surpluses (that is, produced more than they consumed).

   (4) The Russian Federation was the third-largest consumer.

   (5) North America had a surplus (that is, produced more than it consumed).

Questions 7 and 8 refer to Tables 5 and 6. Read each question and choose the correct answer.

Table 5. Top Five Gas Producers,* 2001

United States	22.5
Russian Federation	22.0
Canada	7.0
United Kingdom	4.3
Algeria	3.2

*As a percentage of the world total

Table 6. Top Five Coal Producers,* 2001

United States	26.3
China	24.4
Australia	7.5
India	7.2
South Africa	5.6

*As a percentage of the world total

7. Which country is a top producer of gas **and** coal?

    (1) United States

    (2) China

    (3) Canada

    (4) Australia

    (5) United Kingdom

8. Which of the following statements may be correctly inferred from Tables 5 and 6.

    (1) The United States has a larger share of the world's coal production than of its gas production.

    (2) India produces more coal than Australia does.

    (3) The United States produces less coal than China does.

    (4) Most of the top gas producers are developing nations.

    (5) South Africa produces a larger share of the world's coal than Canada does of the world's gas.

Answers

1. (5)
2. (5)
3. (2)
4. (4)
5. (3)
6. (5)
7. (1)
8. (1)

QUALITY-OF-LIFE INDICATORS

The quality of life in a country can be estimated by looking at the following key statistics, or indicators:

- The rate of population increase
- Infant mortality (the number of infants who die in the first year of life)
- Literacy (the percentage of the adult population that can read and write at a basic level)
- Gross domestic product divided by total population (GDP per capita)
- The percentage of GDP that comes from agriculture

Table 7. Key Quality-of-Life Indicators for Selected Countries, 2001

Country	Population increase per 1000 people	Infant mortality per 1000 births	Literacy	GDP/capita (U.S. $)	GDP from agriculture
A	21.9	80.5	43%	$2000	25%
B	9.2	28.1	82%	$3600	15%
C	16.5	63.2	52%	$2200	25%
D	3.7	5.0	97%	$24 800	3%
E	19.5	20.3	84%	$10 300	14%

Questions

The following questions refer to the preceding passage and Table 7. Read each question and choose the correct answer.

1. Which country listed in Table 7 has the highest infant mortality rate?

    (1) Country A

    (2) Country B

    (3) Country C

    (4) Country D

    (5) Country E

2. Which of the above countries has the lowest rate of population increase?

    (1) Country A

    (2) Country B

    (3) Country C

    (4) Country D

    (5) Country E

3. Which of the following statements may be correctly inferred from Table 7?

    (1) Countries with higher population increases tend to have higher GDP per capita.

    (2) Countries with higher GDP per capita tend to have lower percentages of GDP from agriculture.

    (3) No relationship appears to exist between the rate of population increase and the infant mortality rate.

    (4) Countries with higher literacy rates tend to have higher percentages of GDP from agriculture.

    (5) Countries with higher infant mortality rates tend to have higher GDP per capita.

Answers

1. (1)

2. (4)

3. (2)

Table 8. Human Development Index (HDI) for Selected Countries, 2002

Country	Life expectancy at birth (years)	Adult literacy	GDP/capita ($ U.S.)	HDI
Mexico	73	91%	$9 000	0.796
Togo	52	57%	$1 400	0.493
France	77	100%	$24 200	0.928
Canada	79	99%	$27 800	0.940
Lebanon	73	86%	$4 300	0.755

UNITED NATIONS HUMAN DEVELOPMENT INDEX

The United Nations (UN) publishes a study each year in which it assesses the quality of life of the average member in each of its member nations. It calls this study its human development index (HDI). The HDI has three components:

- Life expectancy at birth
- Adult literacy rate
- GDP/capita

The rates are calculated for each country and placed on an index with a theoretical maximum of 1.000 and a theoretical minimum of 0.000. Table 8 lists the HDI and its components for each of five countries.

Questions

The following questions refer to the preceding passage and Table 8. Read each question and choose the correct answer.

1. In which country is the quality of life the highest?

    (1) Mexico

    (2) Togo

    (3) France

    (4) Canada

    (5) Lebanon

2. Which of the following statements may **not** be correctly inferred from Table 8?

    (1) Togo had the lowest life expectancy of the countries listed.

    (2) Lebanon had the second-lowest adult literacy of the countries listed.

    (3) Canada had the highest figures in every category for the countries listed.

    (4) Mexico had the third-highest GDP per capita of the countries listed.

    (5) France had the second-highest HDI of the countries listed.

Answers

1. (4)

2. (3)

GED Social Studies

Practice Test

PRACTICE TEST

> **Directions:** Read the information below and then answer the related questions. Choose the single best answer to each question.

Questions 1 and 2 refer to the following passage.

While a new political structure was imposed on Upper and Lower Canada by the Act of Union in 1840, the middle decades of the 19th century witnessed significant structural changes in the economies of British North America, resulting partially from developments abroad. The colonies shifted away from their transatlantic links with Britain toward a more continental economy in which the United States figured more prominently. Important strides were taken in improving the St. Lawrence waterway during the 1840s and in building railways after 1850. Immigration remained high. Industrialization began to transform the economy and people's lives. Politically, the greatest challenges consisted of integrating French Canadians into the new political structures, achieving responsible government, and creating new political coalitions.

1. What is the main idea of this passage?

   (1) Canadians were still very dependent on Britain during the mid-19th century.

   (2) Canadians were beginning to extend their transatlantic interests to other European countries besides Britain.

   (3) More and more Canadians were immigrating back to Britain, prompted by British industrialization.

   (4) French Canadians were having more dealings across the Atlantic with Britain.

   (5) The Canadian economy grew more independent of Britain and began to prosper through its dealings in North America.

2. Which of the following is a reason for Canada's economic weaning from Britain?

   (1) New interactions with the United States

   (2) Improvements in the St. Lawrence waterway

   (3) High immigration

   (4) Prominent industrialization

   (5) All of the above

Questions 3 and 4 refer to the following passage.

When he was elected leader of the Liberal Party in 1919, William Lyon Mackenzie King carried the aura of a reformer. He had recently published a book titled *Industry and Humanity*, which proposed several social welfare measures. In office, however, King was a conventional, cautious leader, and the promises of 1919 were largely unfulfilled.

Yet by the 1940s King moved to implement a comprehensive, universal social policy. An unemployment insurance plan was developed in 1940 and expanded in 1945. The old-age pension was extended and increased. Plans were also developed for veterans' housing, educational grants, farm assistance programs, and retraining provisions. Even more ambitious medicare and pension schemes were promised. Although many of those schemes required long and complicated federal and/or provincial negotiations, one program was quickly implemented and entirely within federal jurisdiction—the "Baby Bonus." Each month, every Canadian family would receive a cheque from the federal government based on the number of family members.

Critics argued that the scheme was based on pure political cynicism; others considered it a bribe to the more fecund Quebec. Supporters called the Baby Bonus a much-needed support for the family as well as a sound economic measure (because it directly increased the spending power of all Canadian families). Coincidentally, the federal election was held a few days after every Canadian household received its first cheque.

3. What is the purpose of the first paragraph?

(1) To demonstrate King's early effectiveness as a reformer

(2) To explain why King never became an effective reformer

(3) To show the importance of King's book throughout his political career

(4) To contrast King's early accomplishments with his later effectiveness as a reformer

(5) To downplay King's later achievements

4. What is the importance of the passage's final sentence?

(1) It clarifies that King's plan would have little effect on the election.

(2) It shows how coincidence upset King's plans.

(3) It reveals how poor King's timing was.

(4) It suggests that King developed the Baby Bonus as a means to secure the federal election.

(5) It serves no purpose other than informing the reader of the time of the first cheque's arrival.

Questions 5 and 6 refer to the following table.

Percentage Distribution of Foreign Ownership in Canada, 1920–1960

Year	United States	United Kingdom	Other
1920	44	53	3
1930	61	56	3
1939	60	36	4
1950	76	20	4
1960	75	15	5

5. In which of the indicated years did the U.S. percentage of foreign ownership in Canada reach its highest point?

(1) 1920

(2) 1930

(3) 1939

(4) 1950

(5) 1960

6. Which of the following conclusions may be correctly drawn from the table?

    (1) U.S. ownership rose consistently throughout the period.

    (2) British ownership dropped consistently throughout the period.

    (3) "Other" ownership rose and fell consistently throughout the period.

    (4) British ownership was the highest percentage in all the years indicated.

    (5) There was an overall trend of declining British ownership and increasing U.S. and "other" ownership during the period indicated.

Questions 7 and 8 refer to the following map.

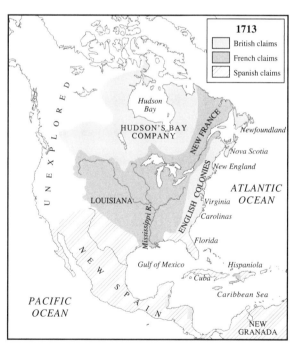

Part of North America after the Treaty of Utrecht, 1713

7. Which of the following is the most significant change to the map of North America that was made by the Treaty of Utrecht?

    (1) Several British colonies along the eastern seaboard of the present-day United States were established.

    (2) The land around Hudson Bay was given to the Hudson's Bay Company.

    (3) France was given present-day Labrador, Quebec, southern Ontario, and the land on both sides of the Great Lakes.

    (4) Nova Scotia and the area between the Hudson's Bay Company's land and present-day Quebec was given to Britain.

    (5) France was given Isle St. Jean.

8. Which of the following events next affected the map of North America by changing ownership of a substantial area of territory, as recognized by the Treaty of Paris in 1763?

    (1) Russian Revolution

    (2) Mexican War

    (3) World War I

    (4) French Revolution

    (5) France's defeat by the British at Quebec

Questions 9 and 10 refer to the following passage and table.

Clause 33 of the Canadian Charter of Rights and Freedoms

Parliament or the legislature of a province may expressly declare an Act of Parliament or of the legislature, as the case may be, that the Act or a provision thereof shall operate notwithstanding a provision included in section 2, or sections 7 to 15 of this Charter.

Subjects of Other Selected Clauses of the Charter

Clause(s)	Subject	Example(s)
2	Fundamental freedoms	Freedom of religion, conscience, etc.
3–5	Democratic rights	Entering, leaving, and remaining in Canada
6	Mobility rights	Living in any province or territory
7–13	Legal rights	Right to a legal counsel; presumption of innocence; freedom from cruel and unusual punishment
16–22	Equality rights	Freedom from discrimination based on sex, age, or mental or physical disability

9. Which of the following laws does clause 33 prevent legislators from passing in an attempt to overrule a right granted in the Charter?

    (1) A law banning a particular religion

    (2) A law banning a Canadian citizen from living in Canada

    (3) A law depriving certain people from access to a lawyer

    (4) A law declaring a person guilty of a crime

    (5) A law authorizing the use of torture on certain people

10. Which prime minister spearheaded the creation of the Charter in 1982 as an integral part of the Canadian constitution?

    (1) John Diefenbaker

    (2) Lester Pearson

    (3) Pierre Trudeau

    (4) Brian Mulroney

    (5) Jean Chrétien

Questions 11 and 12 refer to the following table.

Selected Provincial Populations, 1871 and 1911

Year	British Columbia	Manitoba	Ontario	Quebec	New Brunswick
1871	32 247	25 228	1 620 851	1 191 516	285 594
1911	392 480	461 394	2 527 292	2 005 776	351 889

11. In which province did the population increase the most, in absolute terms, between 1871 and 1911?

  (1) British Columbia

  (2) Manitoba

  (3) Ontario

  (4) Quebec

  (5) New Brunswick

12. In which province did the population increase the most, in percentage terms, between 1871 and 1911?

  (1) British Columbia

  (2) Manitoba

  (3) Ontario

  (4) Quebec

  (5) New Brunswick

Questions 13 and 14 refer to the following passage and cartoon.

The causes of World War I seemed obscure to many Canadians in 1914. Austrian Archduke Franz Ferdinand was shot and killed in Sarajevo (Bosnia) on June 28 by a supporter of Serbian independence. Afterward, few could have predicted that it would lead Canada to join the coalition of Britain, France, and Russia against Germany, Austria-Hungary, and Italy in a four-year war. The following cartoon was published in 1914.

Source: The Brooklyn Eagle, July, 1914

13. If we imagine that the people in the picture are assigned a letter from A to F, from left to right, which country does person D represent?

  (1) Serbia

  (2) Austria-Hungary

  (3) Russia

  (4) Germany

  (5) Britain

14. What message is the cartoonist trying to communicate?

    (1) The war was no country's fault.

    (2) The war was Germany's fault.

    (3) The war was caused by each country's joining in after an enemy had joined the war.

    (4) The war was a good idea to defend the world against tyranny.

    (5) The war was a surprise to all the countries.

Questions 15 and 16 refer to the following passage and cartoon.

In 1959 the Canadian dollar was worth about 1.04 U.S. dollars. But in 1962 the government of John Diefenbaker lowered the value to 0.925 U.S. dollars, or 92½ cents. There was much opposition to this move in Canada at the time, because many saw it as an admission that Canada's economic health was not good. As the following cartoon attests, political cartoonists had a great time with this news item.

15. Which group of people in Canada would have been most likely to support the reduction in value of the Canadian dollar?

    (1) Importers

    (2) Exporters

    (3) Farmers

    (4) Service workers

    (5) Professionals

16. What was the cartoonist saying about the change in value of the Canadian dollar?

    (1) It was a good idea.

    (2) Everyone should support it.

    (3) Everyone should oppose it.

    (4) It is not certain whether it is a good idea or not.

    (5) There is some humour in the event.

Source: Peter Kuch/Winnipeg Free Press, reproduced with permission.

Questions 17 and 18 refer to the following passage and poster.

In the election of 1896, the major political parties presented different visions of Canada's future. The Conservatives, whose election poster is shown, wanted to maintain all the old policies that had been in place for 30 years and to maintain close ties with Canada's traditional friends. The Liberals wanted to strike out in new directions and move closer to nations that were growing in influence in the world. The election poster reproduced here was one of the most memorable from the campaign.

Source: Courtesy of Library and Archives of Canada and Brechin Imaging Services

17. Who is the man being hoisted on the shoulders of his supporters?

   (1) Sir John A. Macdonald

   (2) Sir Wilfrid Laurier

   (3) Sir Robert Borden

   (4) Arthur Meighen

   (5) William Lyon Mackenzie King

18. Which of the following policies would **not** be consistent with the message contained in the poster?

   (1) Continuing with the same leader and prime minister

   (2) Forging closer ties with the United States

   (3) Giving preference to imported goods from Great Britain

   (4) Showing Canada's support for the British Empire

   (5) Showing continuing loyalty to Queen Victoria

Questions 19 and 20 refer to the following passage and map.

Various sailors explored the Canadian Arctic waters. Most were British. They sailed in from the Atlantic Ocean and went as far west as they could, until they were stopped by the landmass or pack ice. The map illustrates some of their voyages of exploration.

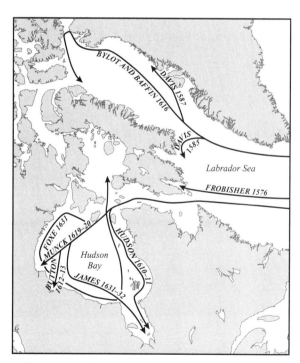

European Explorations to Canada's Arctic Waters, 1585–1632

19. The largest two bays in the Canadian mainland are named after explorers. One is Hudson Bay. What is the other?

    (1) Foxe Bay

    (2) Munk Bay

    (3) Button Bay

    (4) James Bay

    (5) Frobisher Bay

20. A significant driving force behind their explorations was **not** the search for

    (1) a shorter route from Britain to China.

    (2) slaves.

    (3) personal riches.

    (4) riches for their King or Queen.

    (5) personal fame.

Questions 21 and 22 refer to the following passage.

Many forms of business flourish in the free market system. Single owners set up and run small, private companies to sell goods or services to a limited number of customers. However, because some businesses are too large for an individual to run, economic partnerships are set up. Sometimes such businesses grow to become limited partnerships, in which the partners own shares in the company, are employed by it, and look after its day-to-day operations. If the business further expands, it may develop into a public company, in which anyone—including those who neither are employed by it nor have anything to do with its daily func-tioning—may own the company's shares. In this form of business the owners may hand over day-to-day management to a group of individuals who are employed by the company. Public companies are also known as corporations. Some corporations are owned by the government and are called Crown Corporations. In a further stage of development, the business may become so large, sometimes with hundreds of thousands of owners, that it may dominate its market sector and drive out all competition. Such businesses are known as monopolies.

21. Which of the following forms of organizations best describes Air Canada?

    (1) Single-owner company

    (2) Partnership

    (3) Limited partnership

    (4) Public company (corporation)

    (5) Monopoly

22. Which of the following businesses is most likely to be a limited partnership?

    (1) PetroCanada

    (2) A landscaping business run as a part-time endeavour

    (3) A corner variety store

    (4) A firm of three lawyers in a small town

    (5) The Canadian Broadcasting Corporation (CBC)

Questions 23–27 refer to the following graphs.

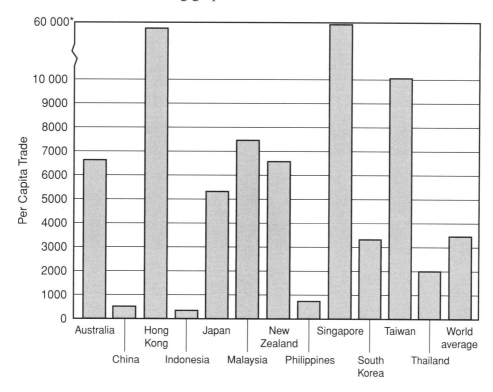

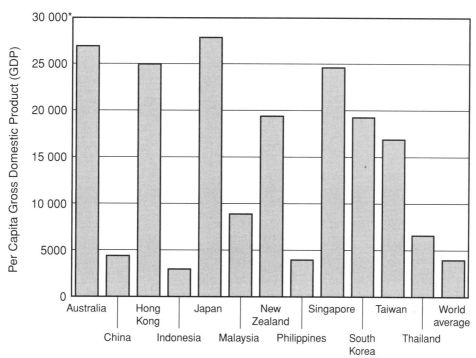

*Amounts are in thousands of U.S. dollars.

Exports and Gross Domestic Product (GDP) per Capita of Selected Countries, 2002

23. Comparing the two graphs, which is the best conclusion?

    (1) There is a direct relationship between trade and GDP per capita.

    (2) All the nations have increased their GDP.

    (3) All the nations exceeded the world average in per capita trade.

    (4) Japan is the leader in both per capita trade and GDP per capita.

    (5) Indonesia ranks lowest in both categories.

24. Which is **not** true about both graphs?

    (1) Both use per-person data.

    (2) Both are in thousands of dollars.

    (3) Both compare the same nations.

    (4) Both are the same type of graph.

    (5) Both use the same year's data.

25. Which economic region of the world is reflected in the graphs?

    (1) East Asia

    (2) All Asia

    (3) Northwest Asia

    (4) All the Pacific

    (5) All ex-British colonies

26. The nation that is increasing its prosperity the most is probably

    (1) Australia.

    (2) Hong Kong.

    (3) Japan.

    (4) Singapore.

    (5) Taiwan.

27. Which is the best way to describe the GDP?

    (1) Total goods and services

    (2) Total national production

    (3) Greater national production

    (4) Government natural production

    (5) Gross national resources

Questions 28–31 refer to the following passage, table, and graph.

Until 1997 this place was a colony of Great Britain. In that year it became a special administrative region of the People's Republic of China. As such, it has greater economic freedom than other regions of China, and it continues to be a dynamic capitalist city. Many of the items exported from and imported through it have their origin or final destination in other regions of China. Natural resources and agricultural land are in very limited supply, and population density is great. About one-seventh the size of Ireland, it has twice that country's population.

Total Area	1040 km²
Population (2002)	7 303 334
Labour force	3 400 000
GDP/capita	$25 000 (U.S. dollars)
GDP growth	1.8%
Inflation rate	−1.6%

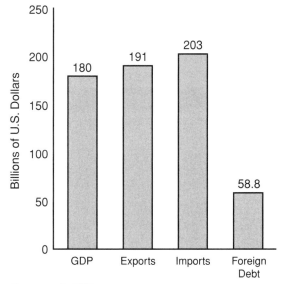

Figures are for 2001.

28. The area being described is

    (1) Australia.

    (2) Northern Ireland.

    (3) Hong Kong.

    (4) Gibraltar.

    (5) Singapore.

29. Which occupation is particularly suited to this area?

    (1) Farmer

    (2) Merchant

    (3) Autoworker

    (4) Teacher

    (5) Tourist guide

30. The statistics contained in the preceding table lead to what conclusion?

    (1) This is a poor nation.

    (2) This is a rich nation.

    (3) The nation is industrially efficient.

    (4) The nation is weak industrially.

    (5) The nation has a one-product economy.

31. The statistics indicate what kind of trade balance?

    (1) Favorable

    (2) Unfavorable

    (3) With excessive debt

    (4) With reasonable debt

    (5) Balanced

Questions 32 and 33 refer to the following passage.

Caucus Standing Rules

1. This caucus shall be governed by Robert's Rules of Order (newly revised), unless the caucus rules provide otherwise.

2. Membership in this caucus is based on both of the following criteria:

    a. . . . being either a member in good standing of the Party or a delegate of the Party (in accordance with the rules of the convention).

    b. . . . being an active member, a retired member, or a professional staff member.

3. Voting privileges shall be extended to all qualified caucus members as defined in section 2.

4. Officers of the caucus shall be the chairperson, vice chairperson, and secretary.

   a. The officers shall be elected by the majority of those persons present and voting.

   b. The officers shall be elected for a two-year term in accordance with the election of the Party officers at the spring convention held in February of the odd-numbered years.

   c. The chairperson shall fill vacancies by appointment, subject to the approval of the Executive Committee.

   d. In the event the chairperson can no longer serve, the secretary shall call an Executive Committee meeting within 30 days. At the meeting the Executive Committee shall appoint a chairperson to serve until the next regularly scheduled election, at which point the caucus will elect a chairperson to fill the unexpired term.

5. Each district will elect one coordinator and one alternate at the spring convention.

32. The presiding officer of the organization is the

   (1) president.

   (2) caucus leader.

   (3) chairperson.

   (4) chief executive.

   (5) chief executive officer.

33. A caucus is part of a

   (1) political party.

   (2) government.

   (3) provincial government.

   (4) national government.

   (5) corporation.

Questions 34–36 refer to the following chart.

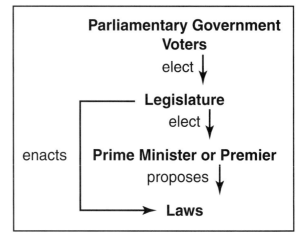

Parliamentary Government

34. In a parliamentary system,

   (1) there is no popular election of the government leader.

   (2) the voters directly create laws.

   (3) the legislature has less power than the prime minister.

   (4) only the prime minister or premier can enact laws.

   (5) only the legislature is responsible for law making.

35. The term *Parliament* comes from the legislature of

    (1) the United States.

    (2) the Soviet Union.

    (3) Great Britain.

    (4) Germany.

    (5) China.

Government Systems Adopted by Various Countries

Parliamentary	Restricted parliamentary	One-party
Canada	Brazil	Syria
United States	Colombia	Algeria
Venezuela	Turkey	Sudan
India	Egypt	Kenya
Spain	Indonesia	Ivory Coast

36. Many legislatures are *bicameral*, which means

    (1) having two political parties.

    (2) being elected by the people.

    (3) being supreme.

    (4) having a two-house system of government.

    (5) constitutional.

Questions 37 and 38 refer to the following passage and table.

A government system falls into one of several categories. One such category is a parliamentary system, in which a number of parties compete for seats in the legislature at free and open elections. A second category is a restricted parliamentary system, in which a number of parties compete for seats, but the powers of the elected officials are limited by strong executive power. In a third category, a one-party system, a single party is permitted to nominate people for the legislature. Individuals may be appointed by an individual or group, or they may be chosen by voters, who have a rather limited choice. The following table illustrates examples of the three systems.

37. What would be the best alternate title for the table?

    (1) World Government Forms

    (2) Sampling of Government Organizations

    (3) Capitalism Versus Communism

    (4) First-World Versus Third-World Government

    (5) Poor Versus Rich Governments

38. One pattern among countries that have adopted the one-party system is that

    (1) all are former British colonies.

    (2) all have kings.

    (3) all are Arabic.

    (4) all are on the Mediterranean Sea.

    (5) all are from the same continent.

Questions 39 and 40 refer to the following passage.

Political systems are constantly changing. Countries collapse and new ones are created.

Until 1989, East Germany was one of the more antidemocratic countries in the world. The government was communist, and all political opposition to it was banned. In that year, the Berlin Wall fell. East and West Germany united into the democratic country of Germany the following year. The old communist system of the East was swept away.

New countries can also be created when regions declare their independence. East Timor is an example of such a country. It sits on the eastern half of the island of Timor, and was part of Indonesia. In 1999, the inhabitants of the region voted to form their own separate country. In 2002, with United Nations support, East Timor became the first new nation formed in the 21st century. Unfortunately, its history since then has not been peaceful, as different groups use force to compete for power.

It is rare for new nations to be created without significant violence and civil war. Nations do not like to have provinces or regions declare their independence. The United States fought a civil war over this issue in the mid-19th century. Majority opinion in Canada today is that Quebec must not be allowed to become an independent nation. In 1980 and 1995, the people of Quebec rejected independence in referendums. (The1995 vote was extremely close.) But the majority of Canadians don't want to see an independent Quebec. Various Canadian governments have tried to grant special terms to Quebec in order to reduce its desire for independence.

39. Which of the following conclusions may be correctly derived from the above passage?

(1) Political systems are always stable and countries never collapse.

(2) East Germany collapsed because it was too democratic.

(3) Nations collapse, but no new ones have been created since the 1960s.

(4) East Timor used to be part of Indonesia.

(5) The United Nations opposes increasing the number of countries in the world.

40. Which of the following conclusions may be correctly derived from the above passage?

(1) New nations are usually created through negotiation without violence.

(2) Nations do not like to have provinces or regions declare their independence.

(3) The United States solved its problems of regions wanting to leave it without violence.

(4) Quebec voted to separate from Canada in a referendum in 1995.

(5) Most Canadians accept that Quebec should be allowed to separate from Canada.

Questions 41 and 42 refer to the following passage.

The idea of a global water shortage seems incredible when 70 per cent of the earth's surface is covered by water. Ninety-eight per cent of that water is salty, however, making it unusable for drinking or agriculture. Desalinization is technically feasible, but it is far too expensive to use anywhere except in a rich, sparsely populated country such as Saudi Arabia. Other options, such as towing icebergs from the poles, are also beyond the means of poor nations.

The scarcity of freshwater for agriculture makes famines more likely every year. The world consumes more food than it produces, yet there are few places to turn for additional cropland. Only by drawing on international stockpiles of grain have poorer countries averted widespread starvation. But those supplies are being depleted. From 1987 to 1989 the number of days the world's surplus of grain would last fell from a 101 to 54. A drought in the U.S. breadbasket could rapidly lead to a global food calamity.

Even if rainfall stays at normal levels, current world food production will be difficult to maintain, much less increase. The food supply has kept pace with population growth only because the amount of land under irrigation has doubled in the past three decades. Now, however, agriculture is losing millions of hectares of this land to the effects of improper watering.

41. World food supply is in danger because

(1) individual people are eating more.

(2) grain-growing nations have been unwilling to share surpluses.

(3) population is growing faster than the surplus of world grain.

(4) irrigated farmland is now being lost.

(5) poor nations waste money on desalination projects.

42. What has enabled the food supply to keep up with population growth?

(1) Towing icebergs

(2) Desalinization

(3) Rainfall

(4) Stockpiling of grain

(5) Irrigation

Question 43 refers to the following illustrations and passage.

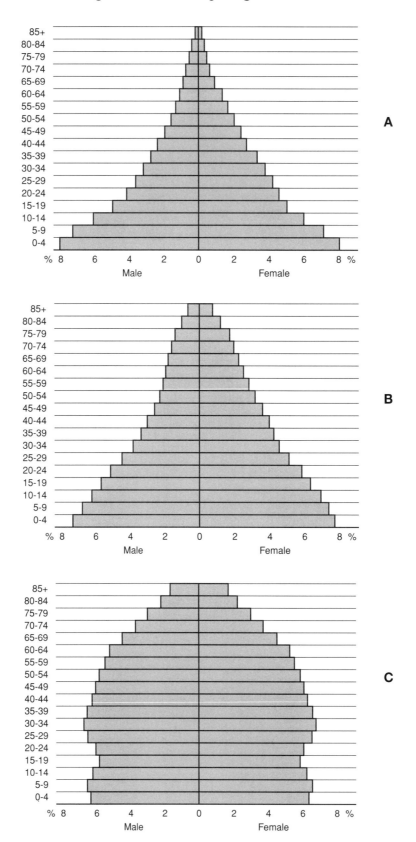

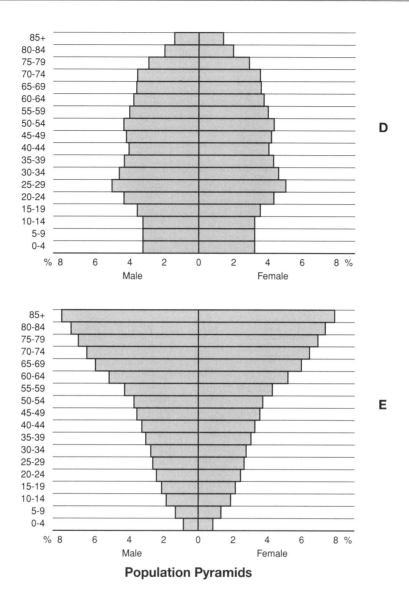

Population Pyramids

Geographers use so-called population pyramids to illustrate the age distribution of individual countries. As shown in the following examples, each age band, represented by a horizontal bar, is a percentage of the total, with males on the left and females on the right.

43. Which of the population pyramids best represents a developed, industrial country like Canada or the United States in the 2000s?

    (1) Pyramid A

    (2) Pyramid B

    (3) Pyramid C

    (4) Pyramid D

    (5) Pyramid E

Questions 44 and 45 refer to the following passage and table.

The various countries of the world may be classified into four basic economic types:

a. Diversified economies

b. Emerging industrial economies

c. Oil resource economies

d. Agricultural economies

Diversified economies have industrial systems of production. Among other features, they tend to be the richest countries in the world.

Country	Population increase per 1000 people	Infant mortality per 1000 births	Literacy (%)	GDP per capita (U.S. dollars)	Percentage of GDP from agriculture
A	3.0	4.5	99	24 400	3
B	11.2	9.4	95	8500	4
C	16.7	95.2	45	1800	32
D	16.0	40.9	84	2900	21
E	8.9	7.7	98	16 100	6

44. Which of the countries is most likely to have a diversified economy?

   (1) Country A

   (2) Country B

   (3) Country C

   (4) Country D

   (5) Country E

45. Which of the countries is most likely to be a developing industrial one?

   (1) Country A

   (2) Country B

   (3) Country C

   (4) Country D

   (5) Country E

Question 46 refers to the following graphs.

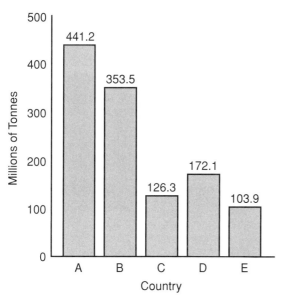

Oil Production for Five Countries, 2000

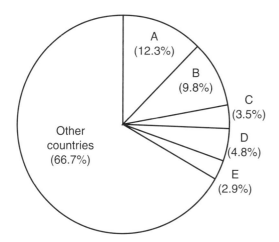

Percentage of World Total Oil Production for Five Countries, 2000

46. Which of the countries is most likely to be Saudi Arabia?

(1) Country A

(2) Country B

(3) Country C

(4) Country D

(5) Country E

Questions 47–49 refer to the following passage and table.

The Human Development Index (HDI) is a measure developed by the United Nations (UN) to compare the quality of life enjoyed by residents in the world's countries. It is based on life expectancy, levels of literacy, and levels of income. Each year the UN publishes a list ranking all the world's countries from the highest level of HDI to the lowest. Another statistic published each year is the number of seats in the legislature (parliament, or equivalent) in each country held by women. The following table is based on the UN's findings for 2002.

HDI Rankings and the Percentage of Seats Held by Women in the Legislatures of Selected Countries, 2002

Country	HDI ranking	Legislative seats held by women (%)
Norway	1	36.4
Australia	2	25.4
Canada	3	23.6
Sweden	4	42.7
Belgium	5	24.9
Ethiopia	158	7.8
Burkina Faso	159	11.0
Burundi	160	14.4
Niger	161	1.2
Sierra Leone	162	8.8

47. Based on the information in the preceding passage, which of the following statements is **not** true about the HDI?

    (1) It includes literacy levels in its measures.

    (2) It is published annually.

    (3) It includes life expectancy in its measures.

    (4) It includes levels of income in its measures.

    (5) Its purpose is to find out which is the best country in the world.

48. Which country listed in the table had the highest percentage of legislative seats held by women?

    (1) Norway

    (2) Sweden

    (3) Canada

    (4) Australia

    (5) Niger

49. What conclusion can be correctly drawn from the preceding table?

    (1) Burundi has a higher percentage of female legislators than Belgium does.

    (2) Countries with a lower percentage of female legislators tend to have higher HDI rankings.

    (3) Sweden has a lower HDI level than Australia does.

    (4) Countries with a higher percentage of female legislators tend to have higher HDI rankings.

    (5) There is no correlation between the percentage of female legislators and HDI levels.

Question 50 refers to the following passage and bar graph.

Various factors—such as regional famines, civil war, and economic dislocation—are expected to increase the migrations of people among the various regions of the world. Current predictions for these migrations are presented in the following bar chart.

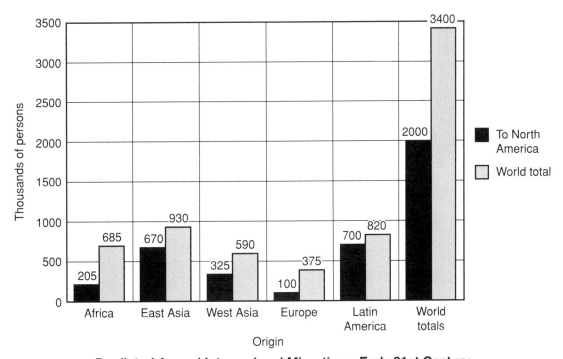

Predicted Annual Interregional Migrations, Early 21st Century

50. Which conclusion may be correctly drawn from the information in the graph?

    (1) North America will receive fewer than half these annual migrations.

    (2) Most of North America's immigrants will come from East Asia.

    (3) Of all the regions, the fewest will come from West Africa.

    (4) The fewest emigrants to North America will come from Europe.

    (5) Approximately 40 per cent of West Asia's emigrants will go to North America.

PRACTICE TEST

ANSWER KEY

1. (5)	14. (3)	27. (1)	40. (2)
2. (5)	15. (2)	28. (3)	41. (4)
3. (4)	16. (5)	29. (2)	42. (5)
4. (4)	17. (1)	30. (3)	43. (4)
5. (4)	18. (2)	31. (2)	44. (1)
6. (5)	19. (4)	32. (3)	45. (2)
7. (4)	20. (2)	33. (1)	46. (1)
8. (5)	21. (4)	34. (1)	47. (5)
9. (2)	22. (4)	35. (3)	48. (2)
10. (3)	23. (5)	36. (4)	49. (4)
11. (3)	24. (4)	37. (2)	50. (4)
12. (2)	25. (1)	38. (5)	
13. (4)	26. (4)	39. (4)	

PRACTICE TEST ANSWERS AND EXPLANATIONS

1. **(5)** The passage focuses on the Canadian colonies' shifting "away from their transatlantic links with Britain toward a more continental economy in which the United States figured more prominently." (1) Because of this, the colonies grew less dependent on Britain. (2 and 3) There is no mention in the passage of the colonies' other European interests or of Canadian immigration to Britain prompted by British industrialization (3). French Canadians were certainly not increasing their dealings with Britain (4).

2. **(5)** Canada's continental economy, in which the United States became more important (1); the improvement of the St. Lawrence waterway (2); high immigration (3); and growing Canadian industrialization (4) are all cited in the passage as reasons for Canada's changed economy. Therefore, all are important reasons for Canada's economic independence.

3. **(4)** Because the passage includes a description of King's later, more vigorous reforms, it is reasonable to assume that the first paragraph serves as a foil to emphasize those later achievements. (1) King's early achievements as a reformer were certainly less than effective. (2) However, reforms he later proposed became realities. (3) King's book is not mentioned during the description of his later reforms. (5) And his early conventionalism does not serve to downplay his later liberalism; the one merely serves to give notice to the other.

4. **(4)** There is certainly some suspicion at the end of the passage that the arrival of the cheque a few days before the election is more than just a coincidence. The passage implies that King had more on his mind than the country's welfare when he timed the distribution of the first Baby Bonus cheque. The timing of the cheque probably helped King's vote immensely; therefore, (1) is certainly wrong. (2) Even if coincidence were involved, it would certainly not have served to "upset" King's election. (3) King's timing was anything but poor. (5) The final sentence of the passage is certainly more than an unbiased conclusion to the issue of the Baby Bonus.

5. **(4)** U.S. ownership in Canada reached 76 per cent in 1950. The percentages for all the other indicated years were lower.

6. **(5)** British ownership fell from 53 per cent to 15 per cent, while U.S. ownership rose from 44 per cent to 75 per cent, and "other" ownership rose from 3 per cent to 5 per cent. (1) In 1939 U.S. ownership was lower than it had been in 1930. (2) In 1930 British ownership was higher than it had been in 1920. (3) "Other" ownership rose in the period indicated. (4) U.S. ownership was the highest in all the years indicated.

7. **(4)** Nova Scotia and the area between the Hudson's Bay Company's land and present-day Quebec were given to Britain by the treaty. This was a major change, because it placed the British on both sides of the French territory in present-day Quebec. All the other solutions listed were in place before 1713.

8. **(5)** France's defeat by the British in Quebec took place in 1759, and the Treaty of Paris (1763) recognized the British claim to Quebec, requiring that a new map be drawn up. All the other events listed took place after the Treaty of Paris. The dates are: (1) 1917, (2) 1846, (3) 1914–1918, and (4) 1789–1815. In addition, none of those events affected the territory indicated on this map.

9. **(2)** Clause 33 can only be used to override sections 2 and 7–15 of the Charter. Rights related to living in Canada are covered in clauses 3–5 and are therefore exempt from clause 33. (1) is covered by clause 2. (3), (4) and (5) are covered by clauses 7–13; clause 33 may be used to overrule those sections of the Charter. Note that clauses 16–22 may not be overruled by the clause 33, but none of the laws listed deals with a matter from these clauses.

10. **(3)** Pierre Trudeau was prime minister from 1968 to 1979 and from 1980 to 1984. The dates of the other prime ministerships are (1) John Diefenbaker, 1957–1963; (2) Lester Pearson, 1963–1968; (4) Brian Mulroney, 1984–1993; and Jean Chrétien, 1993–2003.

11. **(3)** Calculating the absolute increase in population requires subtracting the 1871 population from the 1991 population. This makes Ontario the province that experienced the largest absolute increase (2 527 292 − 1 620 851 = 906 441). The figures for the other provinces are as follows: (1) British Columbia, 392 480 − 32 247 = 360 233; (2) Manitoba, 461 394 − 25 228 = 446 166; (4) Quebec, 2 005 776 − 1 191 516 = 814 260; (5) New Brunswick, 351 889 − 285 594 = 66 295.

12. **(2)** Calculating the percentage increase in population requires subtracting the 1871 population from the 1991 population, dividing the increase by the 1871 population, and multiplying by 100. This makes Manitoba the province that experienced the largest percentage increase: 461 394 − 25 228 = 446 166 ÷ 25 228 × 100 = 1769 per cent. The figures for the other provinces are as follows: (1) British Columbia, 1117 per cent; (3) Ontario, 56 per cent; (4) Quebec, 68 per cent; (5) New Brunswick, 23 per cent.

13. **(4)** Person D represents Germany, as indicated by the style of helmet and the fact that this person appears late in the chain of events that set off the war. (1) Person A represents Serbia, (2) person B represents Austria-Hungary, (3) person C represents Russia, and (5) person E represents France. All these countries joined in after the previous country—an enemy—had joined in the war. Note that person F represents Great Britain, the last major country to join the fighting and Canada's strongest ally in the war.

14. **(3)** The war was caused by the countries joining in, one after the other, when an enemy joined in. (1 and 2) The cartoonist is showing that many countries were to blame. (4 and 5) The cartoon makes no reference to these topics.

15. **(2)** Exporters would be most likely to support the move because it would make Canadian exports cheaper and thus enable them to sell more and make greater profits. (1) Importers would oppose the move because it would make imports more expensive. People would buy fewer imports, and importers would make less money. (3, 4, and 5) Farmers, service workers, and professionals would all be affected in the same way: imports would be more expensive for them, so their standard of living would decline; therefore, they would be likely to oppose the move.

16. **(5)** The "Bunk of Canada" and "Approximately one dollar" labels on the bill, as well as the name "Diefendollar" point to the humour of the event. (1), (2), (3), and (4) are incorrect because there is no real evidence in the cartoon to suggest these conclusions.

17. **(1)** Sir John A. Macdonald was the leader of the Conservative Party beginning with confederation in 1867 and was prime minister from 1867 to 1874 and from 1878 to 1896. He was definitely the "Old Man." The other people listed were all Canadian prime ministers but from later time periods: (2) Sir Wilfrid Laurier, 1896–1911; (3) Sir Robert Borden, 1911–1920; (4) Arthur Meighen, 1920–1921 and 1926; (5) William Lyon Mackenzie King, 1921–1926, 1926–1930, and 1935–1948.

18. **(2)** Forging closer ties with the United States would have been a new element in Canada's international outlook. Canada had always regarded the United States with suspicion, especially after it invaded in 1812, and had not forged close ties in the past. All the other policies listed represent continuations of policies: (1) Macdonald was prime minister; (3) the National Policy provided for preference to imported goods from Great Britain since 1879; (4 and 5) Macdonald was a strong supporter of the British Empire and the monarchy.

19. **(4)** James Bay, the southern extension of Hudson Bay, is named after Captain Thomas James (1593–1653). (1) Foxe, (2) Munk, and (3) Button do not have large bays named after them. (5) Frobisher Bay is named after Martin Frobisher (1535–1594), but it is in Baffin Island, not on the Canadian mainland.

20. **(2)** Slaves were not a particularly valuable commodity at this time, and the populations of these regions were small. (1) The search for what was called the Northwest Passage was a strong driving force because China was one of the richest countries in the world. The passage was discovered in the 20th century and is not really viable. (3, 4, and 5) Fame and riches, including gold, silver, and diamonds, were possible for those who found the Northwest Passage.

21. **(4)** Air Canada is a public company. (1, 2, and 3) Because it has hundreds of thousands of owners, it cannot be any of these kinds of organizations. (5) Because it has many competitors, both domestically and internationally, it is not a monopoly.

22. **(4)** Ownership of the law firm is likely to be restricted to the three lawyers, and probably they are not allowed to sell their shares to anyone else without permission of the other two partners. (1) PetroCanada is a public company. (2) and (3) A part-time landscaping company or a corner variety store is likely to be a single-owner company or perhaps a partnership. (5) The CBC is a Crown Corporation.

23. **(5)** Indonesia ranks the lowest in both trade and GDP among the countries listed. (1) Some variation occurs among nations with high GDP levels and relatively low trade levels. (2) There is no data comparing previous years. (3) Thailand, the Philippines, and Indonesia did not exceed the world average in trade. (4) Japan was not the leader in trade.

24. **(4)** The trade graph is a line graph, and the GDP is a bar graph. All the other statements listed are true. (1) *Per capita* means "per person."

25. **(1)** All areas on the map are in the eastern portion of Asia. (2) Not all of Asia is represented; for example, India and the Persian Gulf are not on the map. (3) Northwest Asia would be either the Persian Gulf area or former Soviet countries. (4) Malaysia and Thailand are as close to the Indian Ocean as they are to the Pacific. (5) Only Australia, Hong Kong, Malaysia, New Zealand, and Singapore were ever British colonies. Japan and Thailand were never colonized by foreigners.

26. **(4)** The per capita trade of Singapore not only is the highest but also exceeds its GDP, which means its people are producing exportable products that bring money back into the nation. Hong Kong is second.

27. **(1)** GDP, the gross domestic product, is defined as the total value of goods and services produced by the nation in a given year. (2) Both products and services must be included in the definition of GDP. The other descriptions listed are not correct.

28. **(3)** The key hint is the country's proximity to China.

29. **(2)** The key data reflect the importance of trade in the country. (1) The statistic on the scarcity of agricultural land rules out farming as a suitable occupation. (3, 4, and 5) No data the conclusion that any of these occupations are suitable.

30. **(3)** Again, the data support good manufacturing and trade, which must be efficient for this country to compete on the world market as well as it does. Exports and imports total $394 billion, more than twice Hong Kong's GDP ($181 billion), meaning that it is a significant

port through which trade passes from one country to another.

31. **(2)** This country imports ($203 billion) more than it exports ($191 billion), giving it an unfavorable trade balance. (4) There is no standard given by which one can judge whether or not this country has a reasonable amount of debt. The other types of trade balance are not supported by the data.

32. **(3)** Rule 4 describes the officers, with chairperson listed first and with the most power. None of the other types of officers are mentioned.

33. **(1)** The rules refer to the "Party" several times. (2, 3, and 4) Although political parties obviously exist to control these governments, they are not covered by caucus rules. (5) Corporations are not mentioned anywhere in the rules.

34. **(1)** As the chart indicates, the voters elect a legislature and the legislators then choose the prime minister or premier. (2) The legislature, not the people, enacts laws. (3) Because it has the power to choose the prime minister, the legislature has more power than the government leader. (4) Only the legislature can create laws; the leader may propose legislation for them to consider. (5) There is a dual function, with the leader proposing laws and the legislature either passing or rejecting them.

35. **(3)** Many nations have copied the form and even the names of the British system, but historically the British pioneered it and named their legislature Parliament. (1) Congress is the American legislature. (2 and 4) The Soviet Union and Germany have their own parlia-

ments elected by the people. (5) China has a communist system, with the party leadership meeting to proclaim policy, and is not a true democratic legislature.

36. **(4)** A bicameral legislature has two houses. The other terms may be characteristics of democracy, but *bicameral* does not define them.

37. **(2)** There is a sampling of both government types and nations with those types. A sampling means it is not an all-inclusive list. (1) Not all government forms are included. Others include despotic military and colonial rule. (3, 4 and 5) These titles imply that the table compares two types of government instead of the three described in its three columns. (3) This title refers to economic, not political, systems.

38. **(5)** All are African states. (1) All are former colonies of various European powers, not just Britain. (2) Most have some form of military rule, with or without kings. (3 and 4) Algeria is Arab and on the Mediterranean; the others are in sub-Saharan Africa.

39. **(4)** The passage states that East Timor was part of Indonesia. The other answers are wrong because: (1) East Germany collapsed. (2) East Germany was not democratic. The passage states that it was antidemocratic. (3) East Timor was created in 2002. (5) The United Nations supported East Timor's becoming an independent country.

40. **(2)** The passage clearly states this. The other answers are wrong because: (1) It is rare for new nations to be created without significant violence and civil war. (3) The United

States solved its problems through civil war. (4) Quebec rejected independence in 1995, although the vote was extremely close. (5) The majority of Canadians don't want to see an independent Quebec.

41. **(4)** The passage states that irrigated land is being lost to improper watering. (1) The passage does not discuss individual food consumption. (2 and 3) Even though the producing nations are sharing their surpluses, the population growth has reduced the world surplus from a 101-day to a 54-day supply. (5) Only rich nations can afford desalination projects.

42. **(5)** The last paragraph clearly states that food supply has kept up with the population growth because of irrigation. (1 and 2) These are mentioned as costly ways to solve the water shortage problem. (3) Rainfall is briefly mentioned as a factor that could hinder food production. (4) Grain stockpiling is a way poorer countries have avoided starvation.

43. **(4)** Countries like Canada and the United States have a relatively small percentage of the population in the age groups under 20, a larger percentage in age groups 20–70, and a significant percentage in the age groups over 70. (1) Pyramid A has a large percentage in the age groups under 20 (showing a large number of live births), followed by a rapid narrowing of the age groups 20–65 (indicating a large number of comparatively early deaths). This pattern is characteristic of an agricultural society. (2) Pyramid B shows a smaller number of births and a slower narrowing, resulting in a larger percentage of children who survive to become adults. This pattern is characteristic of an early developing society. (3) Pyramid C shows a small percentage in the age groups under 20 and a larger percentage in the 20–60

age groups. This pattern is characteristic of a developing country. (5) Pyramid E is an imaginary pattern. Clearly, this country would not survive in its present form, with a small percentage of the population in the childbearing or prechildbearing years, and such a high percentage of people in the older age groups.

44. **(1)** Countries with diversified economies are characterized by low population increases and infant mortality rates, high literacy rates and GDP per capita figures, and a smaller percentage of GDP coming from agriculture. Country A displays all these characteristics.

45. **(2)** Developing industrial countries are characterized by medium population increases and infant mortality rates, relatively high literacy rates and GDP per capita figures, and a small percentage of GDP coming from agriculture. Country B displays all these characteristics.

46. **(1)** Saudi Arabia is the world's largest oil producer. Of all the countries listed, country A produces the most oil (441.2 million tonnes) and thus has the largest percentage of the world's total (12.3 per cent). The other countries are B, United States; C, Canada; D, Mexico; and E, Nigeria.

47. **(5)** The passage does not provide information on the purpose of the HDI, so this statement cannot be said to be true. All the other listed statements are mentioned in the passage and thus are true.

48. **(2)** In 2002, women held 42.7 per cent of Sweden's legislature seats. The other figures are (1) Norway, 36.4 per cent; (3) Canada, 23.6 per cent; (4) Australia, 25.4 per cent; (5) Niger, 1.2 per cent, the lowest figure for all the countries listed.

49. **(4)** All the countries with HDI numbers from 1 to 5 have higher percentages of female legislators than do all the countries with HDI numbers from 158 to 162. (1) Belgium has a higher percentage of female legislators (24.9) than Burundi does (14.4). (3) Sweden has a higher percentage of female legislators (42.7) than Australia does (25.4).

50. **(4)** North America will receive only 100 000 migrants from Europe. If you look at the bars over North America, you will see that the amount from every other region is higher than this. (1) North America will receive almost 59 per cent of the total migrations (2000 ÷ 3400 = 58.8 per cent). (2) Most of North America's migrants (700 000) will come from Latin America. (3) The fewest migrants (100 000) will come from Europe. (5) More than 55 per cent of West Asia's migrants (325 ÷ 590 = 55.6 per cent) will go to North America.

GED Social Studies

Post-Test

POST-TEST

Directions: Read the information below and then answer the related questions. Choose the single best answer to each question.

Questions 1 and 2 refer to the following passage.

Canada's constitution was originally called the British North American Act, 1867. It was renamed as the Constitution Act, 1867, and the document remained in the United Kingdom until the present government brought it within Canada's boundaries in 1982. The constitution had been amended 30 different times before Canada acquired possession of it. The government of Canada can now amend the constitution without the approval of the British Parliament. The document is now known as The Constitution Act, 1982, and it provides Canada with a government that consists of three parts: Her Majesty the Queen, the Senate, and the House of Commons. The latter two branches form the Parliament of Canada.

1. Which of the following represent changes concerning the Constitution Act, 1982?

   (1) It allows the Canadian government to amend the constitution without the approval of the British Parliament.

   (2) It gives Her Majesty the Queen full control over the Parliament of Canada.

   (3) The constitution may now remain within Canada's borders, instead of remaining in Britain.

   (4) Both (1) and (3)

   (5) Both (2) and (3)

2. Which of the following comprise the Parliament of Canada?

   (1) Her Majesty the Queen and the Senate

   (2) Her Majesty the Queen and the House of Commons

   (3) The Senate and the House of Commons

   (4) The Senate and the Cabinet

   (5) The House of Commons and the Cabinet

Questions 3 and 4 refer to the following passage.

Women began receiving the vote during World War I. Beginning in Manitoba and Alberta, the women's suffrage movement gradually succeeded in all provinces except Quebec during the 1920s. Some historians claim that the suffrage movement was less about women's issues than about Anglo-Saxon middle-class Protestant values, which were perceived to be under threat from the mass immigrations of the period.

The war saw women move into different occupations and struggle to open up various professions. The struggle for equality, moreover, continued after the war. The first female member of Parliament in the British Commonwealth, Agnes MacPhail, was elected in 1921. Canada's first women's Olympic contingent was sent to the 1928 games.

On October 18, 1929, an earlier Supreme Court judgment that women were not persons and therefore could not be appointed to the Senate was overturned by the Privy Council. The judgment read in part: "to those who ask why the word [person] would include females, the obvious answer is why should it not?" The judgment went on to state that "the exclusion of women from all public offices is a relic of days more barbaric than ours." Shortly after this judgment, Cairine Wilson was appointed to the Senate by William Lyon Mackenzie King.

3. What does the passage's first paragraph suggest that some historians imply about the women's suffrage movement of the 1920's?

(1) The movement served to place more voting power in the hands of Anglo-Saxon Protestants.

(2) The suffrage movement was exclusively concerned with women's issues.

(3) There were more male immigrants arriving in Canada than females.

(4) World War I only hurt the cause of the women's suffrage movement.

(5) The movement's sole purpose was to bolster Canada's team in the Olympics.

4. Which of the following was **not** a manifestation of the increasing rights of Canadian women?

(1) Women gained the right to vote in public elections.

(2) Women moved into new occupations and professions.

(3) The British Commonwealth elected its first female member.

(4) Canada sent its first women's team to the Olympics.

(5) Women were permitted to fight in the war.

Questions 5–7 refer to the following pie graphs.

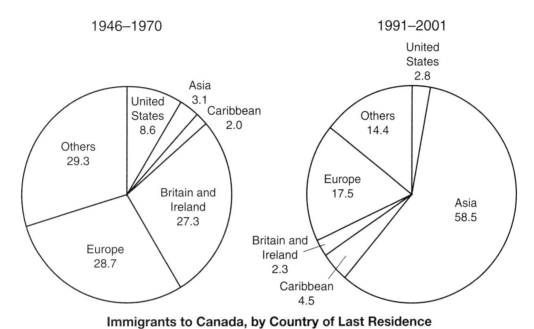

Immigrants to Canada, by Country of Last Residence
(Figures in per cent)

5. From which area did the share of immigrants increase the most between the two periods?

    (1) Britain and Ireland

    (2) United States

    (3) Europe

    (4) Asia

    (5) Caribbean

6. From which area did the share of immigrants decrease the most between the two periods?

    (1) Europe

    (2) United States

    (3) Asia

    (4) Caribbean

    (5) Britain and Ireland

7. By how many percentage points did the total European immigration to Canada decrease between the two periods?

    (1) 56.0

    (2) 28.7

    (3) 2.3

    (4) 36.2

    (5) 24.3

Questions 8 and 9 refer to the following map.

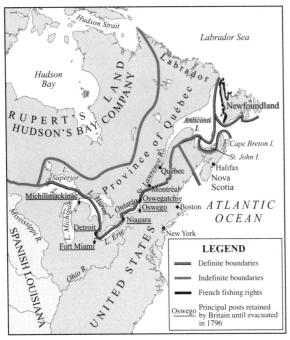

North American Land Settlements as Specified in the Treaties of Paris and Versailles, 1783

8. Which of the following statements was **not** recognized as true before the treaties of Paris and Versailles came into effect?

   (1) The Hudson's Bay Company owned much of the territory around Hudson Bay and James Bay.

   (2) The United States owned the territory south of the Great Lakes around the Ohio River.

   (3) Britain owned the territory of Quebec.

   (4) France had fishing rights off Newfoundland.

   (5) The islands of St. Pierre and Miquelon belonged to France.

9. About this time, loyalists from the United States (opponents of the American Revolution) began to enter the British colonies shown on the map, and they started advocating for political reforms. What was the next major change made to the map by the British in 1791 to accommodate the loyalists' requests?

   (1) St. Pierre and Miquelon were taken from France and given to loyalist settlers.

   (2) St. John's was given back to France.

   (3) The Quebec territory south of the St. Lawrence River was expanded, taking land from New York, Vermont, and Massachusetts.

   (4) Land was taken away from the Hudson's Bay Company and opened for loyalist settlement.

   (5) Quebec was divided into two parts: Upper and Lower Canada.

Question 10 refers to the following bar graph.

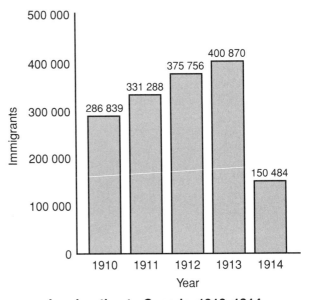

Immigration to Canada, 1910–1914

10. Which of the following events would be likely to account for the number of immigrants in 1914?

    (1) The opening up of new lands to immigrants

    (2) Increased financial aid to immigrants in selected areas

    (3) The arrival of immigrants from new areas such as Ukraine

    (4) The election of a new federal government more sympathetic to immigrants

    (5) The outbreak of the First World War

Questions 11 and 12 refer to the following table.

**Over-representation and
Under-representation in the Male
Labour Force by Selected Groups, 1961**

Occupational category	Percentage of representation over (+) or under (–) the norm	
	British Canadians	Aboriginal people
Professional and financial	+2.0	−7.5
Clerical	+1.3	−5.9
Personal service	−0.9	+1.3
Primary and unskilled	−2.3	+34.7
Agriculture	−1.5	+6.9
All others	+1.4	−29.5

11. Which of the following conclusions can be drawn from the preceding table?

    (1) Aboriginal people were over-represented in professional and financial jobs.

    (2) British Canadians were over-represented in personal service jobs.

    (3) The greatest disparity between the two groups was in the "all others" category.

    (4) The job category in which aboriginal people were closest to being represented according to their numbers in society was in the clerical jobs category.

    (5) British Canadians were over-represented in the clerical jobs category.

12. Which of the following conclusions can be drawn from the preceding table?

    (1) Overall, British Canadians and aboriginal people were equally represented in most job categories.

    (2) The category with the greatest under-representation for aboriginal people was the primary and unskilled category.

    (3) In none of the job categories indicated are both groups either over- or under-represented.

    (4) British Canadians as a group had better jobs because they had a higher level of education.

    (5) Overall, the representation for British Canadians varied more from the norm than did the representation for aboriginal people.

Questions 13 and 14 refer to the following passage and table.

In 1987 the federal government tried (ultimately unsuccessfully) to sign an agreement known as the Meech Lake Accord with the provinces. Among other things, the accord would have amended the constitution to recognize Quebec as "within Canada, a distinct society." The following table summarizes what Anglophones and Francophones thought about issues addressed in the accord.

Poll Regarding Issues in the Meech Lake Accord

Do you think Quebec should be regarded as a distinct society?		
Group	Yes	No
Anglophones	41%	59%
Francophones	58%	42%

Which do you think is more important – the right of Quebec Anglophones to have freedom to communicate in their own language, or the right of Quebec Francophones to preserve their own culture?		
Group	Anglophone freedom of speech	Protection of Francophone culture
Anglophones	72%	28%
Francophones	22%	78%

13. Which of the following statements **cannot** be drawn from the preceding table?

    (1) A bigger percentage of Francophones than Anglophones believed that Quebec should be regarded as a distinct society.

    (2) The percentage of Anglophones opposed to recognizing Quebec as a distinct society was higher than the percentage of Francophones favouring it.

    (3) A majority of Francophones were opposed to recognizing Quebec as a distinct society.

    (4) More than twice as many Anglophones saw their own freedom of speech as the primary issue, compared with those Anglophones who saw protection of Francophone culture as the primary issue.

    (5) The percentage of Anglophones who saw Anglophone freedom of speech as the primary issue was lower than the percentage of Francophones who saw protection of Francophone culture as the primary issue.

14. After the failure of the Meech Lake Accord in 1990, what was the next attempt that the federal government made to reform the constitution and win the Quebec government's support?

    (1) British North America Act

    (2) Bill of Rights

(3)   Canadian Charter of Rights and Freedoms

(4)   Charlottetown Agreement

(5)   Magna Carta

Questions 15 and 16 refer to the following passage and cartoon.

In the period 1896–1911 Canada's prime minister practiced a policy of what he called "sunny ways." The purpose and method of this policy was to bring together all of Canada's various language, religious, and cultural groups and encourage them to work together. The following cartoon, which came from that period, illustrates the "sunny ways" policy.

"HOME, SWEET HOME."

Source: Courtesy of the Library and Archives of Canada and Brechin Imaging Services.

15.   Who is the prime minister described in the passage and pictured in the cartoon?

(1)   Sir John A. Macdonald

(2)   Sir Wilfrid Laurier

(3)   Sir Robert Borden

(4)   Arthur Meighen

(5)   William Lyon Mackenzie King

16.   Which group is not represented as part of Canada's "Home, Sweet Home"?

(1)   Anglicans from England

(2)   Irish people

(3)   Quebeckers

(4)   Aboriginal people

(5)   Ukrainians

Questions 17–19 refer to the following passage and map.

In the early 1870s Canada consisted of seven provinces and a vast area of land in the middle called the Northwest Territories, which was administered by the federal government. Prime Minister Macdonald's greatest fear was that the United States might move north and try to annex much of that land for its expanding population.

Canada might be a transcontinental nation, but it was still not particularly secure. The threat of a possible American invasion required Canada to settle the West as quickly as possible. The following type of sentiment was fairly typical at the time.

The western territories must be settled and settled fast. Even though we have some settlements in place, they are spread out and vulnerable. It is in the vital interest of the federal government to make these areas more attractive to our citizens for settlement. We must make the trip less arduous, and establish solid links of transportation and communication, so that these areas are woven into the fabric of Canada and not of another nation in this hemisphere.

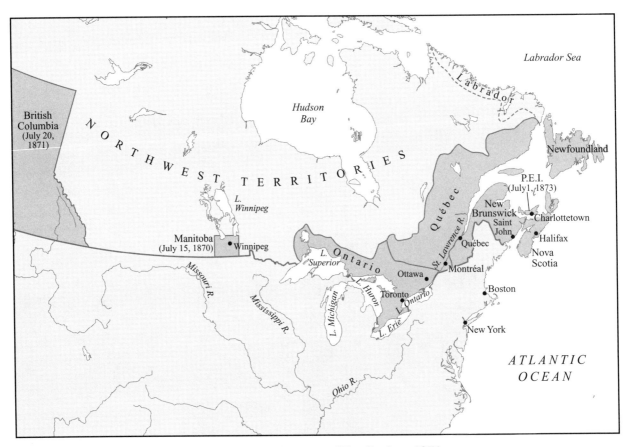

Canada's Provinces and Territories, 1871

17. Look at the map of Canada in 1871. From your knowledge of Canadian history, which of the following was the next place to become a province of Canada?

    (1) Prince Edward Island

    (2) Alberta

    (3) Newfoundland

    (4) Nunavut

    (5) Vancouver Island

18. Look at the final paragraph of the passage above. The writer of this passage would most likely favor

    (1) laissez-faire economics

    (2) government involvement in projects like railroads and mail delivery

    (3) large-scale social programs

    (4) provincial rights

    (5) The British North America (BNA) Act

19. The writer would most likely be a supporter of

    (1) Sir John A. Macdonald

    (2) Sir Wilfrid Laurier

    (3) Henri Bourassa

    (4) the British Crown

    (5) American interests

Question 20 refers to the following passage and pie graphs.

In 1969 the federal government passed the Official Languages Act. This recognized the use of either English or French in the federal government and courts, and put in place programs to promote the use of both languages. The goal of the act was to preserve the use of the two "official languages" in all parts of Canada. Both languages are widely used in the federal government today.

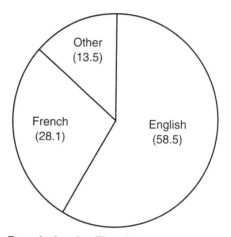

Population by First Language, 1961

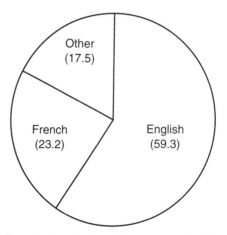

Population by First Language, 2001

20. Based on the passage and the pie graphs, which of the following conclusions can be drawn?

    (1) The act was a success because the use of "other" languages has increased.

    (2) The act was a failure because English is still the most common first language.

    (3) The act was a success because English and French were widely used in 1991, more than 30 years after the act came into effect.

    (4) The act was a failure because French is little used in the federal government outside Quebec and Ontario.

    (5) The act was a success because the use of English increased.

21. The Bank of Canada influences the supply of money in the economy by buying and selling government bonds. Which one of the following would the Bank of Canada use to expand the money supply?

    (1) Sell government bonds

    (2) Buy government bonds

    (3) Raise the bank rate

    (4) Increase secondary reserves of chartered banks

    (5) Increase the fractional reserve rate of chartered banks

22. If a pair of running shorts costs $40 and a pair of sunglasses costs $20, then the opportunity cost of a pair of running shorts will be

    (1) two pairs of sunglasses.

    (2) one pair of sunglasses.

    (3) four pairs of sunglasses.

    (4) one pair of shorts.

    (5) two pairs of shorts.

Questions 23–25 refer to the following table.

Percentage of Jobs in Selected Employment Sectors, 2001

Province	Primary	Manufacturing	Construction	Transport and utilities
Prince Edward Island	13.3	10.7	7.3	3.6
British Columbia	4.6	9.6	5.9	6.2
Saskatchewan	17.3	5.8	5.4	5.8
Manitoba	7.2	11.8	5.0	7.1
Ontario	2.4	16.4	15.5	5.4

23. On the basis of the above table, which province is most likely to be part of the region known as Canada's Industrial Heartland?

    (1) Prince Edward Island

    (2) British Columbia

    (3) Saskatchewan

    (4) Manitoba

    (5) Ontario

24. Based on the given data, which province is likely the least industrialized?

    (1) Prince Edward Island

    (2) British Columbia

    (3) Saskatchewan

    (4) Manitoba

    (5) Ontario

25. Which province has the highest percentage of jobs in the areas of construction and transport & utilities?

    (1) Prince Edward Island

    (2) British Columbia

    (3) Saskatchewan

    (4) Manitoba

    (5) Ontario

Question 26 refers to the following bar graph.

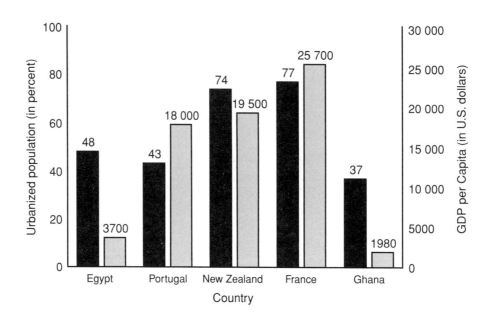

26. Which one of the following conclusions may be drawn from the above bar graph?

(1) The countries with the highest levels of urbanization generally enjoy the highest levels of GDP per capita.

(2) The countries with the highest levels of urbanization consistently have the lowest levels of GDP per capita.

(3) The countries with the lowest levels of urbanization consistently enjoy the highest levels of GDP per capita.

(4) Of the countries shown, Portugal has the highest GDP per capita.

(5) Of the countries shown, Egypt has the lowest urbanization level.

Questions 27–29 refer to the following passage and graphs.

One factor that economists and investors consider in examining a business is how many units of revenue are generated as the number of units of investment increases. This is one measure of a business's efficiency and allows comparison among various companies. The following graphs represent this.

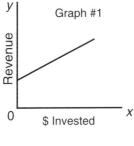

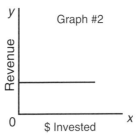

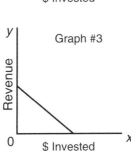

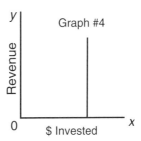

27. In which graph are the most dollars being put in with the least amount of return?

(1) Graph #1

(2) Graph #2

(3) Graph #3

(4) Graph #4

(5) None of the above

28. According to the graphs, which product will never yield more income no matter how much is invested?

(1) Graph #1

(2) Graph #2

(3) Graph #3

(4) Graph #4

(5) None of the above

29. Which of the graphs would a company most like to see in a report about their product?

(1) Graph #1

(2) Graph #2

(3) Graph #3

(4) Graph #4

(5) None of the above

Question 30 refers to the following passage and graph.

In a free market economy, economic stability is rarely present. The economy is either expanding or contracting in the short term, and moving to boom or recession in the longer term. The following theoretical graph illustrates this phenomenon.

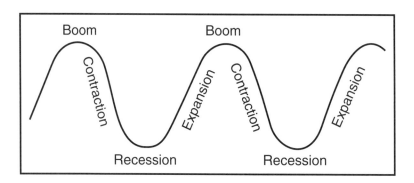

30. In referring to the stages of the cycle above, which would **not** be a factor considered by economists?

   (1) Unemployment figures

   (2) Manufacturing production

   (3) Income levels

   (4) War or peace

   (5) Retail sales

Questions 31 and 32 refer to the following passage.

A constitution is a basic plan for organizing and operating a government. It is also an instrument that formally establishes political institutions and structures, allocates and distributes power, and places restraints and limits to prevent the use, misuse, or abuse of power. A constitution often represents an ideological expression of the ruling elites, as well as being a rationalization and legitimation of their right to exercise and wield power.

Constitutions originate in a number of ways—for example, by 1) fiat, 2) constituent assembly, and 3) evolution. Constitutions that are imposed from above, as in the case of dictatorial regimes, exemplify constitutions by fiat. The American Constitution of 1787, however, originated and developed through a constituent assembly of delegates. The British constitution, on the other hand, is unique. It is not represented by one single document, it has no specific date of origin; it is an amalgam of different sources. As an example of constitutional evolution, the British constitution evolved historically over a long period of time, gradually taking shape and gaining acceptance.

31. Which of the following would best fit the description of a nation's constitution?

   (1) A charter of laws including offenses and punishments for offenders

   (2) A list of provinces with specifics on boundaries separating territory

   (3) A confederation's trade agreements outlined to the last detail

   (4) A statement on the ideals of a nation, as well as the way the government intends to authoritatively carry out those ideals

(5) A list of demands sent from one nation to another, with the hope of convincing the latter of the former nation's worth

32. Which of the following does **not** represent a marked difference between the British constitution and a constitution by constituent assembly?

(1) The British constitution evolved over a long period of time.

(2) The British constitution is the product of many hands.

(3) The British constitution consists of many different documents.

(4) The British constitution is part of a long, historical process.

(5) The British constitution is an amalgam of many historical sources.

Questions 33 and 34 refer to the following cartoon.

Reprinted with permission from the Globe and Mail.

33. What is the cartoonist trying to communicate in the cartoon?

(1) The media (newspapers) expect the Alliance and Tories to join together soon.

(2) The Alliance and Tories will soon join together.

(3) The media (newspapers) think that the Alliance and Tories are the same party.

(4) The Alliance and Tories will take a long time to join together.

(5) The Alliance and Tories are quickly moving closer together.

34. In the cartoon, and in Canadian government generally, what is meant by the term *right*, as used in the newspaper headline?

(1) Communist

(2) Conservative

(3) Terrorist

(4) Liberal

(5) Socialist

Questions 35 and 36 refer to the following table.

**Result of the October 2003 Election in the Riding
of London-Fanshawe, Ontario**

Candidate (Party)	Votes
Khalil Ramal (Liberal)	12 356
Irene Mathyssen (New Democratic)	10 901
Frank Mazzilli* (Progressive Conservative)	10 409
Bryan Smith (Green)	495
Mike Davidson (Family Coalition)	440

* Incumbent

35. What conclusion can be drawn from the table?

(1) Because Smith and Davidson received less than 5 per cent of the votes, they must drop out, and the remaining candidates will run against each other one more time.

(2) Because no one received more than 50 per cent of the total votes cast, another election must be held in this riding.

(3) Because no one received more than 50 per cent of the total votes cast, the first two finishers (Ramal and Mathyssen) must run off in a second election in the riding.

(4) Because Ramal received more votes than any other candidate, he is the new representative for this riding.

(5) Because the difference in the number of votes cast for Ramal and Mathyssen was less than 2000, they will jointly share the duty of representing the riding.

36. The table notes that Mazzilli was the "incumbent." What does that term mean?

(1) He won the previous election.

(2) He was the favourite to win this election.

(3) He had already served one term and was therefore only eligible for one more term.

(4) He had stated that he would not run in another election.

(5) He was regarded by the media as the person likely to come in second, although in fact he came in third.

Questions 37 and 38 refer to the following information from Elections Canada.

Citizenship and Immigration Canada
www.cic.gc.ca

| Français | Home | Contact Us | Help | Search | canada.gc.ca |

Home > Publications

The Department
About Us
The Minister
Media Centre

Visas and Immigration
Visiting Canada
Working Temporarily in Canada
Studying in Canada
Immigrating to Canada
International Adoption
The Refugee System
About Immigration

Living in Canada
Information for Newcomers

Citizenship
Applying for Citizenship
Citizenship Judges
About Citizenship

Resources
Publications
Audits and Evaluations
Research and Statistics

Proactive Disclosure

A Look at Canada

Voting Procedures During an Election Period

1

Voter information card
Electors whose information is in the National Register of Electors will receive a voter information card. This confirms that your name is on the voters list and tells you when and where to vote.

2

I did not get a card
If you do not receive a voter information card, call your local elections office to make sure you are on the voters list. If you do not have the number, call Elections Canada, in Ottawa, at 1 800 463-6868.

3

Advance poll and special ballot
If you cannot or do not wish to vote on election day, you can vote at the advance polls (the dates and location are on your voter information card) or by special ballot.

4

On election day
Go to your polling station. The location is on your voter information card. The poll officials will confirm that you are on the voters list by asking for your name and address and will give you a ballot.

Voting Procedures During an Election Period

(continued)

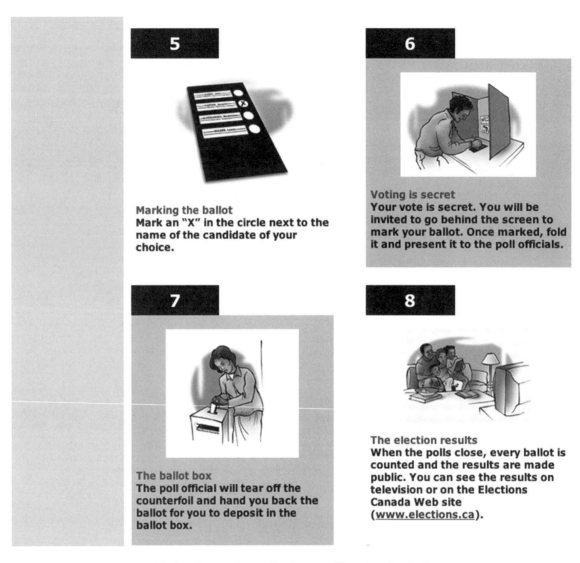

5

Marking the ballot
Mark an "X" in the circle next to the name of the candidate of your choice.

6

Voting is secret
Your vote is secret. You will be invited to go behind the screen to mark your ballot. Once marked, fold it and present it to the poll officials.

7

The ballot box
The poll official will tear off the counterfoil and hand you back the ballot for you to deposit in the ballot box.

8

The election results
When the polls close, every ballot is counted and the results are made public. You can see the results on television or on the Elections Canada Web site (www.elections.ca).

Voting Procedures During an Election Period

37. Which of the following statements about voting in Canadian federal elections is **not** true?

    (1) You indicate your choice of candidate by marking an "X" in the circle next to the appropriate name on the ballot.

    (2) After the polls close, you can watch the results on television as they come in.

    (3) To keep your vote secret, you should go behind the screen to mark your ballot and fold it when handing it back to the poll officials.

    (4) If you do not get a voter information card, you cannot vote in the election.

    (5) If you will not be able to get to the polls to vote on election day, advance polls are available for you to vote before election day.

38. Which is the correct sequence of events in the voting process?

    (1) Fold ballot, mark ballot, receive voter information card, put ballot in box, watch results

    (2) Receive voter information card, fold ballot, put ballot in box, mark ballot, watch results

    (3) Mark ballot, fold ballot, receive voter information card, put ballot in box, watch results

    (4) Watch results, receive voter information card, mark ballot, fold ballot, put ballot in box

    (5) Receive voter information card, mark ballot, fold ballot, put ballot in box, watch results

Questions 39 and 40 refer to the following passage and form.

In Canada the voters list is compiled by elections officials using information from income tax and property tax returns. Normally only people who believe they are eligible but have been left off the voters list, perhaps because they have recently moved to a new constituency, need to register. In most U.S. states people must apply to be initially placed on the voters list. The following form is a typical example of a U.S. voter registration application form.

Print clearly in ink- Use ballpoint pen or marker		State of New Jersey County Commissioners of Registration		76
Qualifications of an Eligible Applicant		**Voter Registration Application**		
You must be a citizen of the United States and by the date of the next elections at least 18 years old and a resident of New Jersey and your county for at least 30 days.	**1**	Check one: ☐ New Registration ☐ Address Change ☐ Name Change		
	2	Last Name First Name Middle Initial	Jr. Sr. II III	
	3	Street Address Where You Live	Apt. #	
	4	City or town	County	Zip Code
The Commissioner of Registration will notify you upon receipt of this form.	**5**	Address Where You Get Your Mail (if different from above)		
	6	Date of Birth- Month, Day, Year **7** Telephone Number (optional)		
The Registration deadline to vote at the next election is 29 days prior to election day.	**8**	Name and Address Of Your Last Voter Registration		
			County	
Check if you wish to be a board worker/poll clerk in future elections. ☐	**9**	Declaration - I swear or affirm that: • I am a U.S. citizen • I live at the above address • I will be at least 18 years old on or before the next election • I am not on parole, probation or serving sentence due to a conviction for an indictable offense under any federal or state laws. • I understand that any false or fraudulent registration may subject me to a fine up to $1,000, imprisonment up to 5 years or both pursuant to R.S. 19:34-1.	For Office Use Only Clerk Registration No. Office Time Stamp	
Check if you are permanently disabled, unable to go to the polls to vote, and wish to receive information on an Absentee Ballot. ☐				
Sign or Mark ➡		Signature or Mark Date		
If applicant is unable to complete this form, print name and address of individual who completed this form.	**10**	Name Address		

39. The registrant in New Jersey must swear to all of the following **except**

   (1) that he/she is a U.S. citizen.

   (2) that he/she will be 21 years old on or before the next election.

   (3) that he/she recognizes that a fraudulent registration is subject to a fine and/or imprisonment.

   (4) that he/she is not on parole, probation, or serving a sentence for an indictable offense.

   (5) that he/she lives at the address indicated.

40. Which of the following is **not** mandatory information that must be provided?

   (1) Date of birth

   (2) Street address

   (3) Name and address of last voter registration

   (4) First and last name

   (5) Telephone number

Questions 41 and 42 refer to the following passage.

Canada is the second-largest country in the world. A simple examination of the latitudes and longitudes of some of its major cities will confirm its size. Vancouver is situated at 49°11' N and 123°11' W. Toronto sits at 43°41' N and 79°38' W. Edmonton is located at 53°19' N and 113°35' W. Halifax is at 44°53' N and 63°31' W. Finally, Windsor is situated at 42°16' N and 82°58' W.

41. Which of these cities is situated furthest from the equator?

   (1) Vancouver

   (2) Toronto

   (3) Edmonton

   (4) Halifax

   (5) Windsor

42. Which of the cities would experience sunset latest?

   (1) Vancouver

   (2) Toronto

   (3) Edmonton

   (4) Halifax

   (5) Windsor

Questions 43–44 refer to the following table.

Percentage of Population by First Language in Selected Canadian Provinces and Territories, 2001

Province/Territory	English	French	Other
Alberta	80.8	2.0	17.2
Northwest Territories	56.7	2.1	41.2
Quebec	8.3	80.9	10.8
British Columbia	76.5	1.5	22.0
Newfoundland and Labrador	98.4	0.4	1.2

43. Which of the following conclusions **cannot** be drawn from the preceding table?

    (1) French is the first language of most people in Quebec.

    (2) The regions with the highest percentage of population having the same first language are Newfoundland and Labrador.

    (3) The region with the highest percentage of the population having languages other than English and French as its first language is the Northwest Territories.

    (4) Fewer people speak native languages in the Northwest Territories than speak English in Quebec.

    (5) English is the first language of most people in British Columbia.

44. Which of the following conclusions can be drawn from the table?

    (1) English is the most popular language in Canada.

    (2) Most people in the listed provinces speak English as their first language.

    (3) In the Northwest Territories most people speak a first language other than English or French.

    (4) A greater proportion of people speak French as a first language in British Columbia than in Alberta.

    (5) French is spoken by a greater proportion of people in the listed provinces and territories than is English.

Questions 45 and 46 refer to the following table.

Area and Population of Canadian Provinces and Territories, 2001

Province	Area (km²)	Population
Alberta	661 848	978 933
British Columbia	944 735	3 907 738
Manitoba	647 797	1 119 583
New Brunswick	72 908	729 498
Newfoundland and Labrador	405 212	512 930
Nova Scotia	55 284	908 007
Ontario	1 076 395	11 410 046
Prince Edward Island	5660	135 294
Quebec	1 542 056	7 237 479
Saskatchewan	651 036	978 933

Territory	Area (km²)	Population
Northwest Territories	1 346 106	37 360
Nunavut	2 093 190	26 745
Yukon	482 443	28 674

45. Which of the following provinces or territories is the least densely populated?

(1) Ontario

(2) Nova Scotia

(3) Yukon

(4) Quebec

(5) Nunavut

46. Which province has the largest area?

(1) Alberta

(2) Quebec

(3) Ontario

(4) Prince Edward Island

(5) Nunavut

Questions 47 and 48 refer to the following passage and table.

A nation's gross domestic product (GDP) is the total of all the goods and services it produces in a year. There are three sectors from which this can be generated: primary (agricultural and other resource-based industries), secondary (manufacturing), and tertiary (sales and services). The following table illustrates some significant differences. All the countries are real ones.

Percentage of GDP Derived from Economic Sectors

Country	Primary		Secondary		Tertiary	
	1960	2000	1960	2000	1960	2000
A	6	3	34	29	60	69
B	39	17	38	50	23	34
C	40	5	19	44	41	52
D	54	17	14	47	32	36
E	65	52	12	11	23	37

47. Which country is most likely to be a developed, industrial nation?

    (1) Country A

    (2) Country B

    (3) Country C

    (4) Country D

    (5) Country E

48. Which country is most likely to have the lowest standard of living?

    (1) Country A

    (2) Country B

    (3) Country C

    (4) Country D

    (5) Country E

Questions 49 and 50 refer to the following passage and bar graphs.

Since the 1970s the worldwide demand for natural gas has climbed substantially. This is in part because natural gas is a cleaner-burning fuel than oil, which is vitally important when there is international agreement that pollution levels must be cut. The bar graphs below measure natural gas production in five of the largest producers.

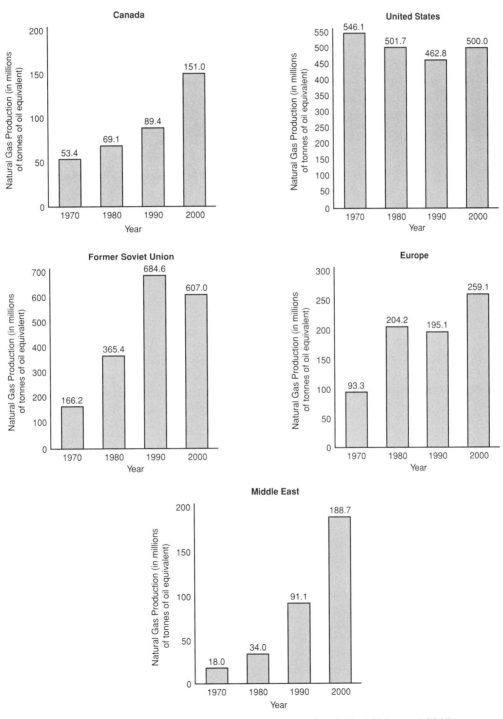

Natural Gas Production in Five Areas, 1970, 1980, 1990, and 2000

49. Which of the areas did not have a higher production in 2000 than in 1970?

    (1) Canada

    (2) United States

    (3) Former Soviet Union

    (4) Europe

    (5) Middle East

50. Which of the following statements is true, based on information in the bar graphs?

    (1) The United States produced more natural gas in 2000 than in 1980.

    (2) The former Soviet Union produced less in 1980 than Europe did.

    (3) The Middle East was the smallest producer in 2000.

    (4) Canada's production more than doubled between 1970 and 2000.

    (5) Europe's production more than tripled between 1970 and 2000.

POST-TEST

ANSWER KEY

1. (4)	14. (4)	27. (3)	40. (5)
2. (3)	15. (2)	28. (2)	41. (3)
3. (1)	16. (4)	29. (4)	42. (1)
4. (5)	17. (2)	30. (4)	43. (4)
5. (4)	18. (2)	31. (4)	44. (2)
6. (5)	19. (1)	32. (2)	45. (5)
7. (4)	20. (3)	33. (4)	46. (2)
8. (2)	21. (2)	34. (2)	47. (1)
9. (5)	22. (1)	35. (4)	48. (5)
10. (5)	23. (5)	36. (1)	49. (2)
11. (5)	24. (3)	37. (4)	50. (4)
12. (3)	25. (5)	38. (5)	
13. (3)	26. (1)	39. (2)	

POST-TEST ANSWERS
AND EXPLANATIONS

1. **(4)** Both the Canadian government's ability to amend the constitution without British Parliamentary consent (1) and the new geographic location of the constitution (3) are cited in the passage as being changes concerning the Constitution Act, 1982. The passage does not state anything about Her Majesty the Queen's relationship with the Canadian Parliament (2). Because (2) is incorrect, (5) must also be incorrect.

2. **(3)** The passage specifically states that of the three parts of the government mentioned in the Constitution Act, 1982 (Her Majesty the Queen, the Senate, and the House of Commons), the latter two branches form the Parliament of Canada. Neither Her Majesty the Queen (1 and 2) nor the Cabinet (4 and 5) comprise the Parliament of Canada.

3. **(1)** The passage states that some historians claim that the suffrage movement was the result of mainstream Canada's fear of being engulfed by the "mass immigrations of the period." The addition of Anglo-Saxon Protestant females' votes would help to stem the tide of control over government decisions. This statement certainly does not indicate that the historians believed the suffrage movement was exclusively concerned with women's issues (2). There is no mention of the ratio of male and female immigrants (3). The passage implies that the war *helped* to establish women's rights, not hindered their establishment; it was during the war era that women began to exercise their right to vote (4). There is no indication that Canadian women's participation in the Olympics

is the primary motivation behind the original women's suffrage movement (5).

4. **(5)** There is no mention in the passage that women were permitted to fight in the war. However, women's right to vote (1), their movement into new occupations and professions (2), the election of the first female member of Parliament in the British Commonwealth (3), and the establishment of the first Canadian women's team in the Olympics (4) are all mentioned in the passage as being manifestations of the increasing rights of Canadian women.

5. **(4)** (1, 2, and 3) Asian immigrants went from a mere 3.1 per cent of immigrants who arrived between 1946 and 1970 to a huge 58.5 per cent of immigrants arriving between 1991 and 2001. The percentage of immigrants from Britain and Ireland dropped, as did the percentages of U.S. and European immigrants. Caribbean immigration increased, but not as much as Asian immigration.

6. **(5)** Britain and Ireland's percentage dropped from 27.3 per cent to 2.3 per cent. (1) Europe's percentage rate dropped only 11.2 per cent. (2) The percentage from the Caribbean increased. (3 and 4) The United States' percentage dropped only slightly, and Asia had a huge increase.

7. **(4)** Total European immigration would include the figures for Britain and Ireland as well as those for Europe. Adding the two differences in percentage rates yields a response

of 36.2 per cent (27.3 + 28.7 − 2.3 − 17.5 = 36.2). (1) 56.0 per cent is the total percentage that Europe represented in the first graph. (2) 28.7 per cent is what Europe represented in the first graph. (3) 2.3 per cent is the number that Britain and Ireland represented in the second graph. (5) The equation will not yield a response of 24.3 per cent if done correctly.

8. **(2)** The United States was not recognized as an independent country until 1783, and the Ohio Valley was claimed by Britain as part of its Quebec colony, won in 1763.

9. **(5)** This change was made in 1791, when the Constitutional Act was introduced. In Upper Canada (present-day Ontario), English land laws operated, and legislatures were elected in both areas. Both those changes helped to satisfy the loyalists. (1) These islands remain French colonies today. (2) This never happened. The island is knows as Prince Edward Island today. (3) This never happened. The Canada-U.S. boundary was not adjusted south of the St. Lawrence River. (4) Loyalists never settled on Hudson's Bay Company land because it was poor for agricultural purposes. The area was purchased by Canada from the company in 1870.

10. **(5)** This event occurred in August 1914. The war disrupted shipping, and immigrants had no way of getting to Canada. All the other events listed would all have increased immigration, not reduced it as the bar graph shows.

11. **(5)** British Canadians were over-represented (by 1.3 per cent) in the clerical jobs category. (1) Aboriginal people were 7.5 per cent under-represented in professional and financial jobs. (2) British Canadians were 0.9 per cent under-represented in the personal service jobs

category. (3) Adding the figures given shows that the disparity in the "all others" category was 30.9 per cent, while the disparity for primary and unskilled workers was 37 per cent. (4) In the clerical jobs category, aboriginal people were 5.9 per cent under-represented. But in the personal service jobs category, they were 1.3 per cent over-represented. Being closer to 0 per cent, this is the closest representation of aboriginal people's numbers in society.

12. **(3)** In every category, when British Canadians are shown as under-represented, aboriginal people are shown as over-represented, and vice versa. (1) There is a wide disparity between the two selected groups. Only in the personal service category is the disparity less than 5 per cent (−0.9 minus +1.3 per cent is a difference of 2.2 per cent). (2) The primary and unskilled jobs category was the one that had the greatest over-representation for aboriginal people. (34.7 per cent). (4) It is impossible to tell from the information in the table if this is correct or incorrect. (5) Representation for British Canadians was in the range of −0.9 per cent to +2.0 per cent. For aboriginal people, the range was −29.5 per cent to +34.7 per cent. In every job category British Canadians were closer to the norm (0 per cent) than were aboriginal people.

13. **(3)** Only 42 per cent of Francophones were opposed. (1) The figures are 58 per cent to 41 per cent. (2) The figures are 59 per cent and 58 per cent. (4) The figures are 72 per cent and 28 per cent. The former figure is more than 2.5 times the latter figure. (5) The figures are 72 per cent and 78 per cent

14. **(4)** The Charlottetown Agreement of 1992 (among the federal, provincial, and territorial governments) was an attempt to reform

the constitution. But it failed when the Canadian population rejected it in a referendum. (1) This was the original Canadian constitution, which came into effect in 1867. (2) This was passed by the federal government in 1962. (3) This was incorporated into the Canadian constitution in 1982. (5) This was an agreement between King John of England and the barons in 1215.

15. **(2)** Sir Wilfrid Laurier was prime minister from 1896 to 1911. He was noted for his "sunny ways" approach. The dates do not fit for the other answers. (1) Sir John A. Macdonald, 1867–1874 and 1878–1896; (3) Sir Robert Borden, 1911–1920; (4) Arthur Meighen, 1920–1921 and 1926; (5) William Lyon Mackenzie King, 1921–1926, 1926–1930, 1935–1948.

16. **(4)** Aboriginal people do not seem to be represented in the cartoon, certainly not the ones who had not converted to Christianity from their traditional beliefs. All the other groups were depicted in the cartoon as follows: (1) "Protestant"; (2) "Catholic" and/or "Protestant"; (3) "French" and "Catholic," or "English" and/or "Protestant"; (5) "Catholic."

17. **(2)** Alberta (with Saskatchewan) became a province in 1905. (1) Prince Edward Island was already a province (since 1873). (3) Newfoundland joined Canada as a province in 1949. (4) Nunavut is a territory, not a province. It became a separate territory in 1999. (5) Vancouver Island is part of British Columbia.

18. **(2)** is the correct answer. By saying it is in the government's vital interest to develop transportation and communication, the writer is making an argument for government involvement in those programs. (1) This is the

opposite of laissez-faire economics, which maintains that government should stay out of business matters. (3) The writer is not advocating large-scale social programs like social security or medicare. (4) By referring to the central government's interests, the writer is probably not a proponent of provincial rights, which would give the provinces more decisions at the expense of the central government. (5) The writer does not mention the British North America Act.

19. **(1)** Macdonald, as Prime Minister, was a strong supporter of building the Canadian Pacific Railway. (2) Laurier, a Liberal, was more concerned with Quebec-Ottawa matters, and (3) Bourassa was more concerned with promoting the Quebec agenda. (4) The British crown had little interest in the development of the railway, and (5) America was more likely to want little settlement in the Canadian west, making it easier to annex the land.

20. **(3)** The Official Languages Act was designed to encourage the use of English and French, and the table shows that they were both still in wide use in 1991. (1) The act was only concerned with the use of English and French. (2) The act was not designed to favour one official language over another. (4) The use of English and French in the federal government outside Ontario and Quebec cannot be ascertained from the information in the passage or pie graphs, but it is probably incorrect. In New Brunswick, for example, where one-third of the population is Francophone, French is widely used in the federal government. (5) Again, the act was not designed to favour one official language over another.

21. **(2)** Through purchasing bonds, the government has put currency in the market. All of

the other answer choices will reduce the money supply. By selling bonds (1), the government is taking money from the purchaser and, therefore, taking money out of the money supply. Answer (3) increases the price of borrowing and therefore reduces the demand for cash. Answers (4) and (5) both mandate the bank to hold more cash out of the market.

22. **(1)** Opportunity cost is an expression of the value of an expenditure in terms of an expenditure that could have been made instead. If you did not buy the shorts, you could have purchased two pairs of sunglasses. Choices (2) and (3) are expressed in terms of the correct good, but in inaccurate amounts. Choice (4) would be the opportunity cost of deciding to buy two pair of sunglasses, and choice (5) is twice the amount of what you purchased.

23. **(5)** Because Ontario has the highest percentage of its Gross Provincial Product coming from manufacturing (16.4 per cent), it is clearly the industrial leader of the provinces illustrated. The others have figures of 5.8 percent to 11.8 percent. (Alternatively, this question could be used as a knowledge question, by eliminating the table.)

24. **(3)** Saskatchewan has the lowest number in the manufacturing section and can therefore be assumed to be the least industrialized. Choices (1), (2), (4), and (5) all have higher scores in the manufacturing category than Saskatchewan.

25. **(5)** The figure for Ontario is 15.5 + 5.4 = 20.9 per cent.

26. **(1)** New Zealand and France have levels of urbanization above 70 percent, and have the highest GDP per capita levels of the countries shown. (2) is false because countries with the highest levels of urbanization generally have the highest levels of GDP per capita. (3) is false because countries with the lowest levels of urbanization generally have the lowest levels of GDP per capita. (4) is false because France's and New Zealand's GDP per capita ($27 500) is higher than Portugal's ($18 000). (5) is false because Ghana's urbanization level (37 percent) is lower than Egypt's (48 percent)

27. **(3)** Graph #3 is correct because more money is being invested (x-axis) and less revenue is coming from it. None of the other graphs show this sort of loss of revenue with more investment dollars.

28. **(2)** Graph #2 demonstrates an increase of investment money but no change in revenue.

29. **(4)** A company would love to see Graph #4 because it shows that the money the company invests never gets any higher but the revenues increase constantly. The only other graph that has a positive yield is #1, but more money must be invested in order to get higher revenue.

30. **(4)** A country's state of war or peace may influence the other factors, but it can have a variety of effects and is not part of the purely economic picture. (1) is used to define whether we are in a recession or not. (2) is also used to present a picture of economic health. (3) is another economic factor which rises during an economic boom. (5) is an important indicator of income, production, and consumer confidence in the economy.

31. **(4)** This statement represents the best summary of the passage's first paragraph, which mentions both the ideological expression of the ruling elite and the system of government that must be developed to carry out those ideals. The passage does not mention a charter of laws (1), list of boundaries (2), trade agreements (3), or international threats (5).

32. **(2)** Although Britain's constitution by evolution is indeed the product of many hands, this does not separate it from a constitution by constituent assembly, which is also the product of many hands. The elements of a long evolution (1), being the composite of many documents (3) and historical sources (5), and being part of a long, historical process (4) are not features of a constitution by constituent assembly.

33. **(4)** The Alliance tortoise refers to "the coming geological era," implying that the two parties will take an extremely long time to get together. Notice also that the two tortoises are moving away from each other, implying that the distance between the Alliance and Tories is getting wider. (3) There is nothing in the newspaper to indicate this. The headline does not suggest that the right (Alliance and Tories) are together, although it does suggest that their attraction to each other is growing. (5) "Quickly" and "geological era" are opposites of each other.

34. **(2)** The term *right* refers to conservative groups like the Progressive Conservatives (Tories) or the Canadian Alliance. (1) Communists are regarded as extreme left. (3) Terrorists are not generally placed on the left–right political spectrum. (4) Liberals are generally regarded as centre-left. (5) Socialists are generally regarded as left.

35. **(4)** In Canadian elections the winner is the "first part the post" (often referred to as FPTP). This means that whoever gets the most votes wins. It is immaterial whether or not the person gets more than 50 per cent of the total votes cast (1, 2, 3, and 5). Some nations hold runoff elections between the top candidates, but Canada does not.

36. **(1)** An incumbent is a person who holds an office and is running in an attempt to win reelection.

37. **(4)** As point 2 on the visual states, if you do not get a voter information card, you should call your local elections office or Elections Canada to make sure you are on the voters list. (1) is shown to be true by point 5 on the visual, (2) by point 8, (3) by point 6, and (5) by point 3.

38. **(5)** On the visual, points 1, 5, 6, 7, and 8 show that this is the correct sequence.

39. **(2)** All of the choices appear in item 9, the list of the registrant's declarations, except a minimum voting age of 21 (2). The legal voting age is 18.

40. **(5)** Item 7 indicates that one's phone number is optional. By implication, all other information listed in choices (1) through (4) is required.

41. **(3)** Edmonton has the highest latitude number, which means it is furthest from the equator. This question is designed to see if students can recognize that the longitude figures are irrelevant to this case; the highest longi-

tude figure, Vancouver (1), shows which city is furthest from the Greenwich Meridian. The question is also designed to see if students can relate latitude figures to the globe, and know what the equator is.

42. **(1)** Vancouver has the highest longitude number, indicating it is situated farthest from the Greenwich Meridian. This question is designed to see if students recognize that the latitude figures do not pertain. Since the other cities are situated to the east of Vancouver, they experience sunset earlier.

43. **(4)** This conclusion cannot be deduced from the table because figures for native languages are not specifically given. The other answers can be validated from the table: (1) 80.9 percent, (2) 98.4 percent, (3) 41.2 percent, and (5) 76.5 percent.

44. **(2)** The table shows that English is the majority language in all the places listed, with the exception of Quebec. (1) The most popular language in the whole country cannot be determined on the basis of only the five places listed. (3) English is the most popular first language in the Northwest Territories. (4) A greater proportion (2.0 per cent) have French as their first language in Alberta than in British Columbia (1.5 per cent). (5) It is obvious from the table that English is spoken by a greater proportion of people in four of the five places listed.

45. **(5)** If you divide Nunavut's population by its area (26 745 ÷ 2 093 190), you get a population density of 0.01 persons per km². The other places have higher population densities: (1) Ontario, 10.6; (2) Nova Scotia, 16.4; (3) Yukon, 0.03; (4) Quebec, 5.8.

46. **(2)** Quebec is the correct response. Its area is 1 542 056 km². (1) The area of Alberta is 661 848 km². (3) The area of Ontario is 1 076 395 km². (4) The area of Prince Edward Island is only 5660 km², the smallest of all the areas listed. (5) Although the area of Nunavut (2 093 190 km²) is greater than that of Quebec, Nunavut is a territory, not a province.

47. **(1)** Country A represents Canada, a developed and industrial nation. Such nations are characterized by low and falling percentages in the primary sector (6 per cent to 3 per cent), moderate and falling percentages in the secondary sector (34 per cent to 29 per cent), and high and rising percentages in tertiary sector (60 per cent to 69 per cent). (2) Country B represents China, and (3) country C represents South Korea. They are not considered developed, industrial nations because their tertiary sectors are too small. (4) Country D represents Indonesia, which has a high primary percentage, a growing secondary percentage, and a low a tertiary percentage. (5) Country E represents Ethiopia, which has a high primary percentage, a low and stable secondary percentage, and a low tertiary percentage.

48. **(5)** Country E (Ethiopia) is the correct answer. Its high primary percentage (52 per cent) indicates an agricultural and undeveloped economy. Because greater wealth tends to be developed in the secondary sector (where Ethiopia is very low at 11 per cent) and in the tertiary sector (where it is comparatively low at 37 per cent), Ethiopia is the most likely nation to have a low standard of living.

49. **(2)** U.S. production in 1990 (500.0) was lower than its 1970 production (546.1). (1) Canada's production rose from 53.4 .to 151.0. (3) The Former Soviet Union's production rose from 166.2 to 607.0. (4) Europe's production rose from 93.3 to 259.1. (5) The Middle East's production rose from 18.0 to 188.7.

50. **(4)** Canada's production rose by a factor of 2.83 (151.0 ÷ 53.4 = 2.83). (1) The United States produced less (500.0) in 2000 than in 1980 (501.7). (2) In 1980 the Former Soviet Union produced more (365.4) than did Europe (204.2). (3) In 2000 Canada (151.0) produced less than the Middle East (188.7). (5) Europe's production rose by a factor of more than 2.7 (259.1 ÷ 93.3 = 2.77) between 1970 and 2000.

GED Social Studies

Pre-Test Answer Sheet

1. ① ② ③ ④ ⑤
2. ① ② ③ ④ ⑤
3. ① ② ③ ④ ⑤
4. ① ② ③ ④ ⑤
5. ① ② ③ ④ ⑤
6. ① ② ③ ④ ⑤
7. ① ② ③ ④ ⑤
8. ① ② ③ ④ ⑤
9. ① ② ③ ④ ⑤
10. ① ② ③ ④ ⑤
11. ① ② ③ ④ ⑤
12. ① ② ③ ④ ⑤
13. ① ② ③ ④ ⑤
14. ① ② ③ ④ ⑤
15. ① ② ③ ④ ⑤
16. ① ② ③ ④ ⑤
17. ① ② ③ ④ ⑤
18. ① ② ③ ④ ⑤
19. ① ② ③ ④ ⑤
20. ① ② ③ ④ ⑤
21. ① ② ③ ④ ⑤
22. ① ② ③ ④ ⑤
23. ① ② ③ ④ ⑤
24. ① ② ③ ④ ⑤
25. ① ② ③ ④ ⑤

26. ① ② ③ ④ ⑤
27. ① ② ③ ④ ⑤
28. ① ② ③ ④ ⑤
29. ① ② ③ ④ ⑤
30. ① ② ③ ④ ⑤
31. ① ② ③ ④ ⑤
32. ① ② ③ ④ ⑤
33. ① ② ③ ④ ⑤
34. ① ② ③ ④ ⑤
35. ① ② ③ ④ ⑤
36. ① ② ③ ④ ⑤
37. ① ② ③ ④ ⑤
38. ① ② ③ ④ ⑤
39. ① ② ③ ④ ⑤
40. ① ② ③ ④ ⑤
41. ① ② ③ ④ ⑤
42. ① ② ③ ④ ⑤
43. ① ② ③ ④ ⑤
44. ① ② ③ ④ ⑤
45. ① ② ③ ④ ⑤
46. ① ② ③ ④ ⑤
47. ① ② ③ ④ ⑤
48. ① ② ③ ④ ⑤
49. ① ② ③ ④ ⑤
50. ① ② ③ ④ ⑤

GED Social Studies

Practice Test Answer Sheet

1. ① ② ③ ④ ⑤
2. ① ② ③ ④ ⑤
3. ① ② ③ ④ ⑤
4. ① ② ③ ④ ⑤
5. ① ② ③ ④ ⑤
6. ① ② ③ ④ ⑤
7. ① ② ③ ④ ⑤
8. ① ② ③ ④ ⑤
9. ① ② ③ ④ ⑤
10. ① ② ③ ④ ⑤
11. ① ② ③ ④ ⑤
12. ① ② ③ ④ ⑤
13. ① ② ③ ④ ⑤
14. ① ② ③ ④ ⑤
15. ① ② ③ ④ ⑤
16. ① ② ③ ④ ⑤
17. ① ② ③ ④ ⑤
18. ① ② ③ ④ ⑤
19. ① ② ③ ④ ⑤
20. ① ② ③ ④ ⑤
21. ① ② ③ ④ ⑤
22. ① ② ③ ④ ⑤
23. ① ② ③ ④ ⑤
24. ① ② ③ ④ ⑤
25. ① ② ③ ④ ⑤
26. ① ② ③ ④ ⑤
27. ① ② ③ ④ ⑤
28. ① ② ③ ④ ⑤
29. ① ② ③ ④ ⑤
30. ① ② ③ ④ ⑤
31. ① ② ③ ④ ⑤
32. ① ② ③ ④ ⑤
33. ① ② ③ ④ ⑤
34. ① ② ③ ④ ⑤
35. ① ② ③ ④ ⑤
36. ① ② ③ ④ ⑤
37. ① ② ③ ④ ⑤
38. ① ② ③ ④ ⑤
39. ① ② ③ ④ ⑤
40. ① ② ③ ④ ⑤
41. ① ② ③ ④ ⑤
42. ① ② ③ ④ ⑤
43. ① ② ③ ④ ⑤
44. ① ② ③ ④ ⑤
45. ① ② ③ ④ ⑤
46. ① ② ③ ④ ⑤
47. ① ② ③ ④ ⑤
48. ① ② ③ ④ ⑤
49. ① ② ③ ④ ⑤
50. ① ② ③ ④ ⑤

GED Social Studies

Post-Test Answer Sheet

1. ① ② ③ ④ ⑤
2. ① ② ③ ④ ⑤
3. ① ② ③ ④ ⑤
4. ① ② ③ ④ ⑤
5. ① ② ③ ④ ⑤
6. ① ② ③ ④ ⑤
7. ① ② ③ ④ ⑤
8. ① ② ③ ④ ⑤
9. ① ② ③ ④ ⑤
10. ① ② ③ ④ ⑤
11. ① ② ③ ④ ⑤
12. ① ② ③ ④ ⑤
13. ① ② ③ ④ ⑤
14. ① ② ③ ④ ⑤
15. ① ② ③ ④ ⑤
16. ① ② ③ ④ ⑤
17. ① ② ③ ④ ⑤
18. ① ② ③ ④ ⑤
19. ① ② ③ ④ ⑤
20. ① ② ③ ④ ⑤
21. ① ② ③ ④ ⑤
22. ① ② ③ ④ ⑤
23. ① ② ③ ④ ⑤
24. ① ② ③ ④ ⑤
25. ① ② ③ ④ ⑤

26. ① ② ③ ④ ⑤
27. ① ② ③ ④ ⑤
28. ① ② ③ ④ ⑤
29. ① ② ③ ④ ⑤
30. ① ② ③ ④ ⑤
31. ① ② ③ ④ ⑤
32. ① ② ③ ④ ⑤
33. ① ② ③ ④ ⑤
34. ① ② ③ ④ ⑤
35. ① ② ③ ④ ⑤
36. ① ② ③ ④ ⑤
37. ① ② ③ ④ ⑤
38. ① ② ③ ④ ⑤
39. ① ② ③ ④ ⑤
40. ① ② ③ ④ ⑤
41. ① ② ③ ④ ⑤
42. ① ② ③ ④ ⑤
43. ① ② ③ ④ ⑤
44. ① ② ③ ④ ⑤
45. ① ② ③ ④ ⑤
46. ① ② ③ ④ ⑤
47. ① ② ③ ④ ⑤
48. ① ② ③ ④ ⑤
49. ① ② ③ ④ ⑤
50. ① ② ③ ④ ⑤

INSTALLING REA's TEST*ware*®

SYSTEM REQUIREMENTS

Pentium 75 MHz (300 MHz recommended) or a higher or compatible processor; Microsoft Windows 98 or later; 64 MB Available RAM; Internet Explorer 5.5 or higher.

INSTALLATION

1. Insert the GED Canadian Social Studies TEST*ware*® CD-ROM into the CD-ROM drive.

2. If the installation doesn't begin automatically, from the Start Menu choose the RUN command. When the RUN dialog box appears, type d:\setup (where *d* is the letter of your CD-ROM drive) at the prompt and click OK.

3. The installation process will begin. A dialog box proposing the directory "Program Files\REA\CA_GED_SS" will appear. If the name and location are suitable, click OK. If you wish to specify a different name or location, type it in and click OK.

4. Start the GED Canadian Social Studies TEST*ware*® application by double-clicking on the icon.

REA's GED Canadian Social Studies TEST*ware*® is **EASY** to **LEARN AND USE**. To achieve maximum benefits, we recommend that you take a few minutes to go through the on-screen tutorial on your computer.

SSD ACCOMMODATIONS FOR STUDENTS WITH DISABILITIES

Many students qualify for extra time to take the GED, and our TEST*ware*® can be adapted to accommodate your time extension. This allows you to practice under the same extended-time accommodations that you will receive on the actual test day. To customize your TEST*ware*® to suit the most common extensions, visit our website at *www.rea.com/ssd*.

TECHNICAL SUPPORT

REA's TEST*ware*® is backed by customer and technical support. For questions about **installation or operation of your software**, contact us at:

> **Research & Education Association**
> **Phone: (732) 819-8880 (9 a.m. to 5 p.m. ET, Monday–Friday)**
> **Fax: (732) 819-8808**
> **Website: www.rea.com**
> **E-mail: info@rea.com**

Note to Windows XP Users: In order for the TEST*ware*® to function properly, please install and run the application under the same computer administrator-level user account. Installing the TEST*ware*® as one user and running it as another could cause file-access path conflicts.

Your Test-Day Checklist

- [ ] Get a good night's sleep. Tired test-takers consistently perform poorly.

- [ ] Wake up early.

- [ ] Dress comfortably. Keep your clothing temperature appropriate. You'll be sitting in yout test clothes for hours. Clothes that are itchy, tight, too warm, or too cold take away from your comfort level.

- [ ] Eat a good breakfast.

- [ ] Take these with you to the test center:
  - Several sharpened No. 2 pencils. Pencils are not provided at the test center.
  - A ballpoint pen
  - Admission ticket
  - Two forms of ID. One must be a current, government-issued identification bearing your photograph and signature.

- [ ] Arrive at the test center early. Remember, many test centers do not allow you into a test session after the test has begun.

- [ ] Compose your thoughts and try to relax before the test.

Remember that eating, drinking, and smoking are prohibited. Calculators, dictionaries, textbooks, notebooks, briefcases, and packages are also prohibited.